THE UNIVERSE AND OUR PLACE IN IT

THE OUTER PLANETS

Edited by
Nicholas Faulkner and Erik Gregersen

Britannica Educational Publishing
IN ASSOCIATION WITH
ROSEN
EDUCATIONAL SERVICES

Published in 2019 by Britannica Educational Publishing (a trademark of Encyclopædia Britannica, Inc.) in association with The Rosen Publishing Group, Inc.
29 East 21st Street, New York, NY 10010

Distributed exclusively by Rosen Publishing.
To see additional Britannica Educational Publishing titles, go to rosenpublishing.com.

Britannica Educational Publishing
J.E. Luebering: Executive Director, Core Editorial
Andrea R. Field: Managing Editor, Compton's by Britannica

Rosen Publishing
Nicholas Faulkner: Editor
Brian Garvey: Series Designer / Book Layout
Cindy Reiman: Photography Manager

Library of Congress Cataloging-in-Publication Data

Names: Faulkner, Nicholas, editor. | Gregersen, Erik, editor.
Title: The outer planets / edited by Nicholas Faulkner and Erik Gregersen.
Description: New York : Britannica Educational Publishing, in Association with Rosen Educational Services, 2019 | Series: The universe and our place in it | Audience: Grades 7–12. | Includes bibliographical references and index.
Identifiers: LCCN 2018014222| ISBN 9781508105992 (library bound) | ISBN 9781508105985 (pbk.)
Subjects: LCSH: Outer planets—Juvenile literature. | Solar system—Juvenile literature.
Classification: LCC QB659 .O974 2018 | DDC 523.4—dc23
LC record available at https://lccn.loc.gov/2018014222

Manufactured in the United States of America

Photo credits: Cover (top), p. 1 Carlos Fernandez/Moment/Getty Images; cover (bottom) Vadim Sadovski/Shutterstock.com; back cover © iStockphoto.com/lvcandy; p. 10 Photo NASA/JPL/Caltech (NASA photo # PIA01324); p. 14 Photo NASA/JPL/Caltech (NASA photo # PIA01193); p. 16 NASA/JPL-Caltech/SwRI/MSSS/Betsy Asher Hall/Gervasio Robles; p. 17 Photo NASA/JPL/Caltech (NASA photo # PIA00857); p. 19 (left and right) NASA/SWRI/MSSS/Gerald Eichstadt/Sean Doran; pp. 23, 68-69 Encyclopædia Britannica, Inc.; pp. 24, 38, 65, 92, 100, 112 NASA/JPL; p. 29 AURA/STScI/NASA/JPL; p. 36 JPL/NASA/Brown University; p. 40 Photo NASA/JPL/Caltech (NASA photo # PIA00704); p. 44 Photo NASA/JPL/Caltech (NASA photo # PIA01627); pp. 47, 71, 72, 74 NASA/JPL/Space Science Institute; p. 51 Photo AURA/STScI/NASA/JPL (NASA photo # PIA01464, STScI-PRC94-53); p. 70 NASA, ESA/Hubble Heritage Team (STScI/AURA); p. 73 B.A. Smith/National Space Science Data Center; pp. 77, 98, 115 Jet Propulsion Laboratory/National Aeronautics and Space Administration; p. 89 Erich Karkoschka, University of Arizona, Tuscon, and NASA; p. 91 NASA, ESA, L. Sromovsky (University of Wisconsin, Madison), H. Hammel (Space Science Institute), and K. Rages (SETI); p. 93 NASA/Caltech/JPL; p. 94 U.S. Geological Survey/NASA/JPL; p. 106 NASA/JPL/Caltech; interior pages background (blue triangles) DiamondGraphics/Shutterstock.com.

CONTENTS

INTRODUCTION

Of the eight planets in our solar system, Jupiter, Saturn, Uranus, and Neptune are called the outer planets. They are much larger than the inner planets and have deep gaseous atmospheres. Because of this, they're sometimes nicknamed the gas giants. Since Jupiter, being the largest, is the outstanding representative of this group, the four outer planets are also known as the Jovian, or Jupiter-like, planets.

The outer planets have no solid surfaces. Jupiter and Saturn consist mainly of liquid and gaseous hydrogen and helium; Uranus and Neptune have melted ices and molten rock as well as hydrogen and helium. All the outer planets are less than twice as dense as water. In fact, Saturn's density is so low that it would float if put in water.

The inner planets (Mercury, Venus, Earth, and Mars) formed at temperatures too high to allow the abundant volatile substances—those with comparatively low freezing temperatures—such as water, carbon dioxide, and ammonia to condense to their ices. They therefore remained small, rocky bodies. In contrast, the large low-density, gas-rich outer planets formed at distances beyond what astronomers have dubbed the "snow line," the minimum radius from the Sun at which water ice could have condensed. With the outer planets, the accretion of icy planetesimals produced objects with masses 10 times that of Earth, sufficient to cause the gravitational collapse of the surrounding gas and dust in the solar nebula. These planets grew so large that their composition approached that of the Sun itself, with hydrogen and helium the dominant elements.

Each of the outer planets has a magnetic field, a ring system, and many known moons, with more likely to be discovered. Most of the known moons move around their respective planets in the same direction that the planets orbit the Sun. The moons are extremely diverse, representing a wide range of environments. Jupiter is orbited by Io, a body wracked by intense volcanism, while Saturn's largest moon, Titan—a body larger than Mercury—exhibits a primitive atmosphere denser than that of Earth. Triton moves in a retrograde orbit around Neptune—that is, opposite to the direction of the planet's orbit around the Sun—and features plumes of material rising through its tenuous atmosphere.

This book explores the characteristics of each of the outer planets and their moons. Jupiter is the most massive of the solar system (more than 1,300 Earths would fit inside it) and the fifth in distance from the Sun. It is a world of extreme and complex weather patterns, including an orange-red oval called the Great Red Spot, a long-lasting storm system that is bigger across than Earth. Jupiter is one of the brightest objects in the night sky, and only the Moon, Venus, and sometimes Mars are more brilliant.

Saturn is easily visible to the unaided eye as a nontwinkling point of light. It is a planet girded by extraordinary rings composed of dusty chunks of ice and are more complex than the rings of any other planet in our solar system. Saturn is arguably the most sublime object in the solar system.

Uranus is the seventh planet in distance from the Sun and the least massive of the solar system's Jovian planets. It is a dazzling blue-green world with an atmosphere of hydrogen, helium, and methane, and winds that are several times stronger than Earth's.

Neptune, the eighth planet from the Sun, is the smallest in diameter of the four outer planets. It is a stormy, windswept world with a vivid blue hue. Its highly active atmosphere is surprising, since it receives so little sunlight to power its weather systems.

Each of the outer planets is a unique and exotic world. As scientists gain the ability to further explore these distant neighbours, we will have a better understanding of the history and formation of our solar system and of our own planet.

CHAPTER 1

GIANT JUPITER

Jupiter is the most massive planet of the solar system. When ancient astronomers named the planet Jupiter for the Roman ruler of the gods and heavens (also known as Jove), they had no idea of the planet's true dimensions, but the name is appropriate, for Jupiter is larger than all the other planets combined. It takes nearly 12 Earth years to orbit the Sun, and it rotates once about every 10 hours, more than twice as fast as Earth; its colourful cloud bands can be seen with even a small telescope. It has a narrow system of rings and almost 70 known moons, one larger than the planet Mercury and three larger than Earth's Moon. Some astronomers speculate that Jupiter's moon Europa may be hiding an ocean of warm water—and possibly even some kind of life—beneath an icy crust.

Given Jupiter's large proportion of hydrogen and its huge mass, it has been traditional to assume that the planet formed by condensation from the primordial solar nebula. This hypothesis implies that the elements should all

Crescent view of Jupiter, a composite of three images taken by Voyager 1 on March 24, 1979.

be present on Jupiter in the same proportions that they occur in the Sun. However, the most recent evidence indicates that the elemental proportions on Jupiter differ from the solar values.

Current models for Jupiter's origin suggest instead that a solid core of about 10 Earth masses formed first as a result of the accretion of icy planetesimals. This core would have developed an atmosphere of its own as the planetesimals released gases during accretion. As the mass of the core increased, it would have become capable of attracting gases from the surrounding solar nebula, thus accumulating the huge hydrogen-helium envelope that constitutes Jupiter's atmosphere and fluid mantle. The accumulating envelope would have mixed with the outgassed atmosphere from the core. Thus, the presently observed enrichment of the most abundant heavy elements in this envelope, compared with solar values, reflects the concentration of such elements in the core.

Jupiter has an internal heat source; it emits more energy than it receives from the Sun. The pressure in its deep interior is so high that the hydrogen there exists in a fluid metallic state. This giant has the strongest magnetic field of any planet, with a magnetosphere so large that, if it could be seen from Earth, its apparent diameter would exceed that of the Moon. Jupiter's system is also the source of intense bursts of radio noise, at some frequencies occasionally radiating more energy than the Sun. Despite all its superlatives, however, Jupiter is made almost entirely of only two elements, hydrogen and helium, and its mean density is not much more than the density of water.

Knowledge about the Jovian system grew dramatically after the mid-1970s as a result of explorations by three spacecraft missions—Pioneers 10 and 11 in 1973–74, Voyagers 1 and 2 in 1979, and the Galileo orbiter and probe, which arrived at Jupiter in December 1995. The Pioneer spacecraft served as scouts for the Voyagers, showing that the radiation environment of Jupiter was tolerable and mapping out the main characteristics of the planet and its environment. The greater number and increased sophistication of the Voyager instruments provided so much new information that it was still being analyzed when the Galileo mission began. The previous missions had all been flybys, but Galileo released a probe into Jupiter's atmosphere and then went into orbit about the planet for intensive investigations of the entire system until September 2003.

In July 2016, the Juno orbiter arrived at Jupiter for a mission expected to last two years. In February 2018, it completed its tenth orbit of Jupiter and went on to explore the planet's south pole. There it discovered massive cyclones unlike any other in solar system. In March 2018, Juno discovered that Jupiter's winds run deep into its atmosphere.

Other looks at the Jovian system were provided in late 2000 and early 2001 by the flyby of the Cassini spacecraft on its way to Saturn and in 2007 by the flyby of the New Horizons spacecraft on its way to Pluto. Observations of the impacts of the fragmented nucleus of Comet Shoemaker-Levy 9 with Jupiter's atmosphere in 1994 also yielded information about its composition and structure.

JUPITER BY THE NUMBERS

Jupiter has an equatorial diameter of about 143,000 kilometres (88,900 miles) and orbits the Sun at a mean distance of 778 million km (483 million miles). Of special interest are the planet's low mean density of 1.33 grams per cubic cm—in contrast with Earth's 5.52 grams per cubic cm—coupled with its large dimensions and mass and short rotation period. The low density and large mass indicate that Jupiter's composition and structure are quite unlike those of Earth and the other inner planets.

Three rotation periods, all within a few minutes of each other, have been established. The two periods called System I (9 hours 50 minutes 30 seconds) and System II (9 hours 55 minutes 41 seconds) are mean values and refer to the speed of rotation at the equator and at higher latitudes, respectively, as exhibited by features observed in the planet's visible cloud layers.

Jupiter has no solid surface; the transition from the gaseous atmosphere to the fluid interior occurs gradually at great depths. Thus, the variation in rotation period at different latitudes does not imply that the planet itself rotates with either of these mean velocities. In fact, the true rotation period of Jupiter is System III (9 hours 55 minutes 29 seconds). This is the period of rotation of Jupiter's magnetic field, first deduced from Earth-based observations at radio wavelengths and confirmed by direct spacecraft measurements. This period, which has been constant for 30 years of observation, applies to the massive interior of the planet, where the magnetic field is generated.

THE ATMOSPHERE AND THE GREAT RED SPOT

Even a modest telescope can show much detail on Jupiter. The region of the planet's atmosphere that is visible from Earth contains several different types of clouds that are separated both vertically and horizontally. Changes in these cloud systems can occur over periods of a few hours, but an underlying pattern of latitudinal currents has maintained its stability for decades. It has become traditional to

Computer-generated visualization of a portion of Jupiter's equatorial cloud layers, simulating a view from between layers.

describe the appearance of the planet in terms of a standard nomenclature for its alternating dark bands, called belts, and bright bands, called zones. The underlying currents, however, seem to have a greater persistence than this pattern. For example, the south equatorial belt has faded away several times and has even totally disappeared (most recently in 2010), only to reappear months or years later.

The close-up views of Jupiter transmitted to Earth by spacecraft reveal a variety of cloud forms, including many elliptical features reminiscent of cyclonic and anticyclonic storm systems on Earth. All these systems are in motion, appearing and disappearing on time scales that vary with their sizes and locations. Also observed to vary are the pastel shades of various colours present in the cloud layers—from the tawny yellow that seems to characterize the main layer, through browns and blue-grays, to the well-known salmon-coloured Great Red Spot, Jupiter's largest, most prominent, and longest-lived feature.

Jupiter has no solid surface—hence, no topographic features—and the planet's large-scale circulation is dominated by latitudinal currents. The lack of a solid surface with physical boundaries and regions with different heat capacities makes the persistence of these currents and their associated cloud patterns all the more remarkable. The Great Red Spot, for example, moves in longitude with respect to all three of the planet's rotation systems, yet it

Jupiter's south pole, as seen by the Juno spacecraft.

does not move in latitude. The strongest thermal emission is detected from blue-gray or purple areas that occur in the equatorial region of the planet. Observations from Juno showed that the poles are covered in swirling Earth-sized storms.

The true nature of Jupiter's unique Great Red Spot was still unknown at the start of the 21st century, despite extensive observations from the Voyager, Galileo, and Juno spacecrafts. On a planet whose cloud patterns have lifetimes often counted in days, the Great Red Spot has been continuously observed since 1878 and may even be the same storm that was observed from 1665 to 1713. From its maximum extent of about 48,000 km (30,000 miles) in the late 19th century, the spot has been shrinking, and since 2012 the spot, once decidedly oval, has become more circular and has been shrinking at an accelerated rate of 900

False-colour mosaic of two of the long-lived white ovals south of the Great Red Spot.

km (580 miles) per year. Its present size is about 16,350 km (10,159 miles) wide—large enough to accommodate Earth easily. These huge dimensions are probably responsible for the feature's longevity and possibly for its distinct colour.

The rotation period of the Great Red Spot around the planet does not match any of Jupiter's three rotation periods. It shows a variability that has not been successfully correlated with other Jovian phenomena. Voyager observations revealed that the material within the spot circulates in a counterclockwise direction once every seven days, corresponding to superhurricane-force winds of 400 km (250 miles) per hour at the periphery. The interior of the spot is remarkably tranquil, with no clear evidence for the expected upwelling (or divergence) of material from lower depths.

The Great Red Spot, therefore, appears to be a huge anticyclone, a vortex or eddy whose diameter is presumably accompanied by a great depth that allows the feature to reach well below and well above the main cloud layers. The Red Spot is heating Jupiter's upper atmosphere from below and making it hundreds of degrees hotter than would be expected from solar heating alone. The spot extends about 320 km (200 miles) into Jupiter's atmosphere.

COMPOSITION OF JUPITER'S CLOUDS

Jupiter's clouds are formed at different altitudes in the planet's atmosphere. Except for the top of the Great Red Spot, the white clouds are the highest, with cloud-top temperatures of about 120 kelvins (K; −240 °F, or −150 °C). These white clouds consist of frozen ammonia crystals and are thus analogous to the water-ice cirrus clouds in Earth's atmosphere. The tawny clouds that are widely distributed over the planet occur at lower levels. They appear to form at a temperature of about 200 K (−100 °F, −70 °C), which suggests that they probably consist of condensed ammonium hydrosulfide and that their colour may be caused by other ammonia-sulfur compounds such as ammonium

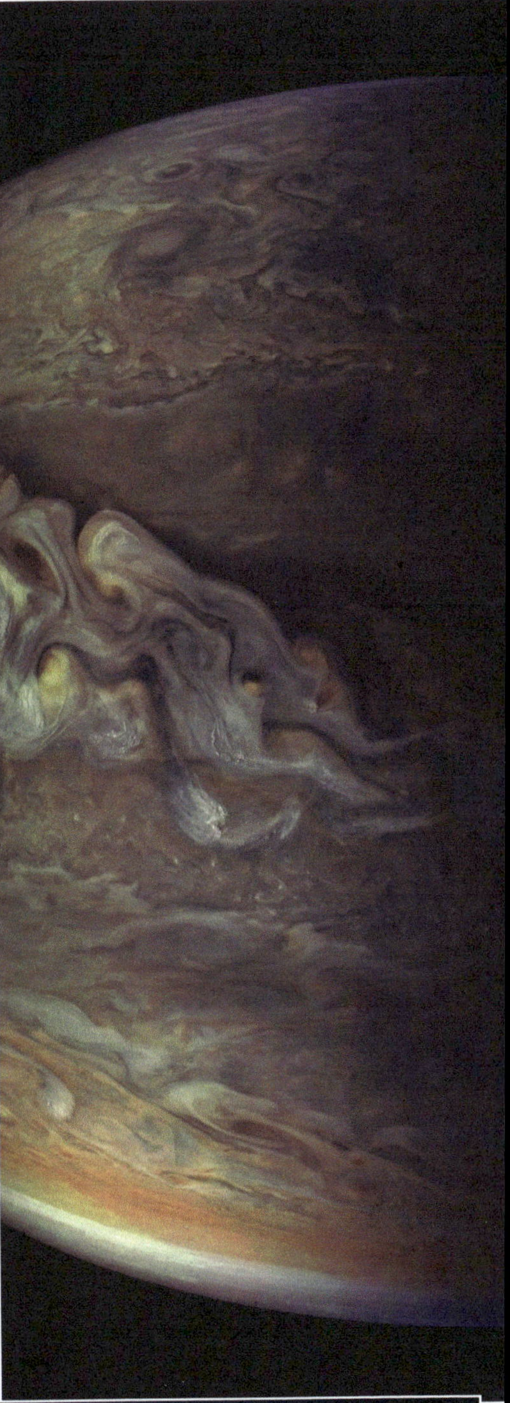

Two views of Jupiter's clouds. Left: the south tropical zone. The small white clouds are composed of water and ammonia ice. Right: waves of clouds.

polysulfides. Sulfur compounds are invoked as the likely colouring agents because sulfur is relatively abundant in the cosmos and hydrogen sulfide is notably absent from Jupiter's atmosphere above the clouds.

Jupiter is composed primarily of hydrogen and helium. Under equilibrium conditions—allowing all the elements present to react with one another at an average temperature for the visible part of the Jovian atmosphere—the abundant chemically active elements are all expected to combine with hydrogen. Thus, it was surmised that methane, ammonia, water, and hydrogen sulfide would be present. Except for hydrogen sulfide, all these compounds have been found by spectroscopic observations from Earth.

The apparent absence of hydrogen sulfide can be understood if it combines with ammonia to produce the postulated ammonium hydrosulfide clouds. Indeed, hydrogen sulfide was detected at lower levels in the atmosphere by the Galileo probe. The absence of detectable hydrogen sulfide above the clouds, however, suggests that the chemistry that forms coloured sulfur compounds (if indeed there are any) must be driven by local lightning discharges rather than by ultraviolet radiation from the Sun. In fact, the causes of the colours on Jupiter remain undetermined, although investigators have developed several viable hypotheses.

At still lower depths in the atmosphere, astronomers expect to find water-ice clouds and water-droplet clouds, both consisting of dilute solutions of ammonium hydroxide. Nevertheless, when the probe from the Galileo spacecraft entered Jupiter's atmosphere on December 7, 1995, it failed to find these water clouds.

CHARACTERISTICS OF THE ATMOSPHERE

The presence of methane and ammonia in Jupiter's atmosphere was detected by absorption spectroscopy in the 1930s, while hydrogen was detected for the first time in 1960. (Although 500 times more abundant than methane, molecular hydrogen has much weaker absorption lines because it interacts only very weakly with electromagnetic waves.) Subsequent studies led to a growing list of new constituents, including the discovery of the arsenic compound arsine in 1990.

Galileo's probe carried a mass spectrometer that detected the constituent atoms and molecules in the atmosphere by first charging them and then spreading them out with a magnetic field according to their masses. This technique had the advantage that it could measure noble gases like helium and neon that do not interact with visible and infrared light. As the probe descended through the atmosphere on its parachute, its spectrometer also studied variations in abundance with altitude. This experiment finally detected the previously missing hydrogen sulfide, which was found to be present even lower in the atmosphere than anticipated. Evidently this cloud-forming gas, like ammonia and water vapour, was depleted in the upper part of the hot spot by the aforementioned downdraft. It was not possible to measure oxygen, because this element is bound up in water, and the probe did not descend into the hot spot deeply enough to reach the atmospheric region where this condensable vapour is well-mixed.

The elemental abundances in Jupiter's atmosphere can be compared with the composition of the Sun. If, like the Sun, the planet had formed by simple condensation from the primordial solar nebula that is thought to have given birth to the solar system, their elemental abundances should be the same. A surprising result from the Galileo probe was that all the globally mixed elements that it could measure in the Jovian atmosphere showed the same approximately threefold enrichment of their values in the Sun, relative to hydrogen. This has important implications for the formation of the planet. Spectroscopy from Earth reveals a large spread in the values of other elements (phosphorus, germanium, and arsenic) not measured by the probe. The abundances of the gases from which these elemental abundances are derived depend on dynamical phenomena in Jupiter's atmosphere—principally chemical reactions and vertical mixing.

In addition to measuring atmospheric composition, the Galileo probe carried instruments to measure both the temperature and pressure during its descent into the Jovian atmosphere. Notably, temperatures higher than the freezing point of water (273 K, 32 °F, 0 °C) were measured at pressures just a few times greater than sea-level pressure

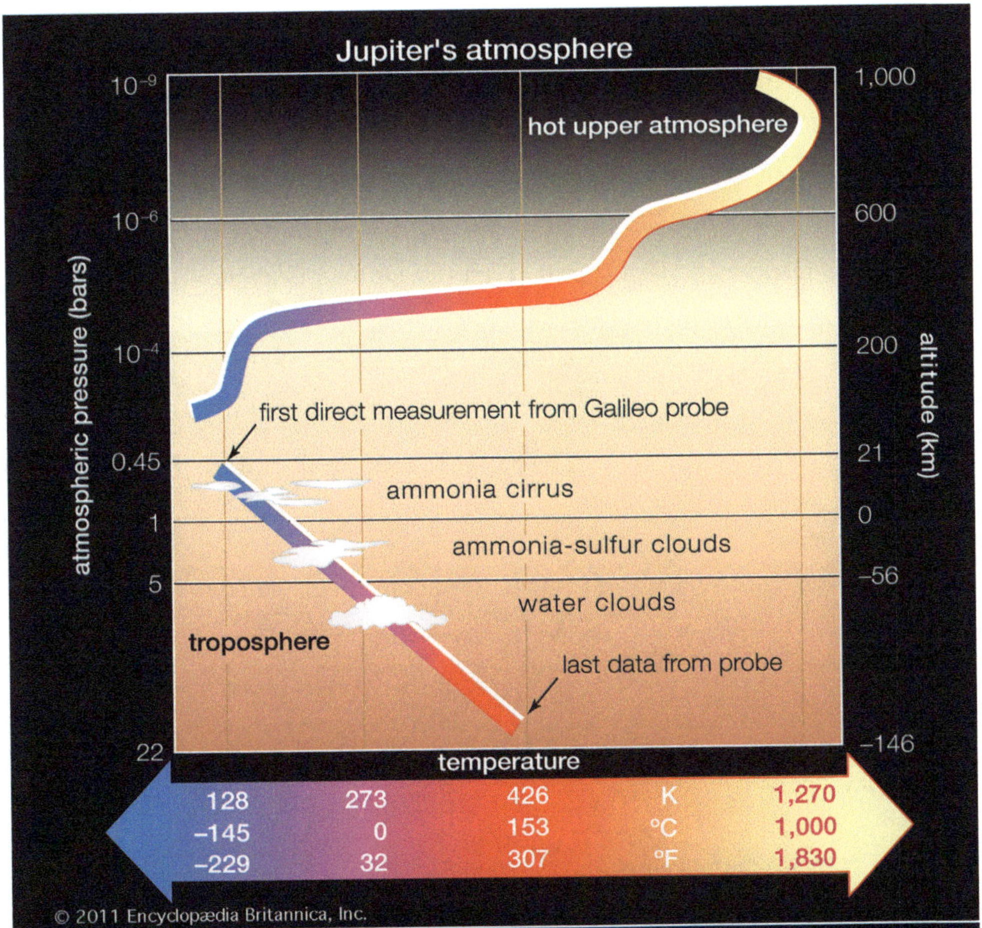

Profile of Jupiter's atmosphere as deduced from accelerometer data and direct measurements collected by the Galileo spacecraft's probe.

COMET SHOEMAKER-LEVY 9

In 1994 Comet Shoemaker-Levy 9, which had been discovered the previous year, crashed into Jupiter's atmosphere after breaking up into more than 20 fragments. The successive explosions were observed by telescopes on Earth's surface, the Earth-orbiting Hubble Space Telescope, and the Galileo spacecraft en route to Jupiter. Only Galileo saw the explosions directly because they occurred on the back side of Jupiter as seen from Earth. Nevertheless, the fireballs produced by the largest fragments rose above the planet's limb, and the resulting black smudges in

The impact of a fragment of Comet Shoemaker-Levy 9 as observed in four images taken by the Galileo spacecraft on July 22, 1994.

Jupiter's cloud layers were visible even in small telescopes as Jupiter's rotation brought them into view. Spectroscopic studies revealed that the impacts had produced or delivered many chemicals such as water, hydrogen cyanide, and carbon monoxide, substances that exist on Jupiter but in much smaller concentrations. The excess carbon monoxide and hydrogen cyanide remained detectable in the upper atmosphere several years after the event. In addition to its intrinsic interest, the collision of a comet with Jupiter stimulated detailed studies of the effects that cometary impacts would have on Earth.

In 2009 a dark spot similar to those left behind by the fragments of Comet Shoemaker-Levy 9 appeared near the south pole of Jupiter. Since only one spot was seen, it was believed that the impacting body was a single body—either a comet or an asteroid—rather than a chain of fragments.

on Earth (about one bar). This is mainly a consequence of Jupiter's internal energy source, although some warming would occur just through the trapping of infrared radiation by the atmosphere via a process comparable to Earth's greenhouse effect.

The formation of complex organic molecules in Jupiter's atmosphere is of great interest in the study of the origin of life. The initial chemical processes that gave rise to living organisms on Earth may have occurred in transient microenvironments that resembled the present chemical composition of Jupiter, although without the enormous amounts of hydrogen and helium. Thus, Jupiter may well represent a vast natural laboratory in which the initial steps toward the origin of life are being pursued again and again. Determining how complex prelife chemical processes can become under such conditions constitutes one of the most fascinating problems confronting any program of space exploration.

JUPITER'S MAGNETIC FIELD AND MAGNETOSPHERE

The nonthermal radio emissions are the natural result of trapped charged particles interacting with Jupiter's magnetic field and ionosphere. Interpretation of these observations led to a definition of the basic characteristics of the planet's magnetic field and magnetosphere that was shown to be remarkably accurate by direct exploration of the vicinity of Jupiter by the Pioneer and Voyager spacecraft. The basic magnetic field of the planet is dipolar in nature, generated by a hydromagnetic dynamo that is driven by convection within the electrically conducting outer layers of Jupiter's interior. The magnetic field strength is about 7.8 gauss, compared with about 0.5 gauss at Earth's surface. The axis of the magnetic dipole is offset by a tenth of Jupiter's equatorial radius of 71,500 km (44,400 miles) from the planet's rotational axis, to which it is indeed inclined by 10°. The orientation of the Jovian magnetic field is opposite to the present orientation of Earth's field, such that a terrestrial compass taken to Jupiter would point south.

The magnetic field dominates the region around Jupiter in the shape of an extended teardrop. The round side of the teardrop faces the Sun, where the Jovian field repels the solar wind, forming a bow shock at a distance of about 3 million km (1.9 million miles) from the planet. Opposite the Sun, an immense magnetotail stretches out to the orbit of Saturn, a distance of 650 million km (404 million miles), which is almost as far as Jupiter's distance from the Sun. These dimensions make Jupiter's magnetosphere the largest permanent structure in the solar system, dwarfing the Sun's diameter of 1.4 million km (870,000 miles). Within this huge region, the most striking activity is generated by the moon Io. An electric current of approximately five million amperes flows in the magnetic flux tube linking Jupiter and Io. This satellite is also the source of a toroidal cloud of ions, or plasma, that surrounds its orbit.

THE AURORAS OF JUPITER

Just as charged particles trapped in the Van Allen belts produce auroras on Earth when they crash into the uppermost atmosphere near the magnetic poles, so do they also on Jupiter. Cameras on the Voyager and Galileo spacecraft succeeded in imaging ultraviolet auroral arcs on the nightside of Jupiter. The Hubble Space Telescope also captured images of far-ultraviolet auroras on the planet's dayside. In addition, Earth-based observations have recorded infrared emissions from H_3^+ ions at both poles and imaged the associated polar auroras. Evidently protons (hydrogen ions, H^+) from the magnetosphere spiral into the planet's ionosphere along magnetic field lines, forming the excited H_3^+ ions as they crash into the atmosphere dominated by molecular hydrogen. The resulting emission produces the auroras. It is observable from Earth at wavelengths where methane in Jupiter's atmosphere has very strong absorption bands and thereby suppresses the background from reflected sunlight. The relation of the ultraviolet and infrared auroras, the detailed interaction of Io's flux tube with Jupiter's ionosphere, and the possibility that ions from the torus of plasma around Io's orbit are impinging on the planet's atmosphere remain active topics of research.

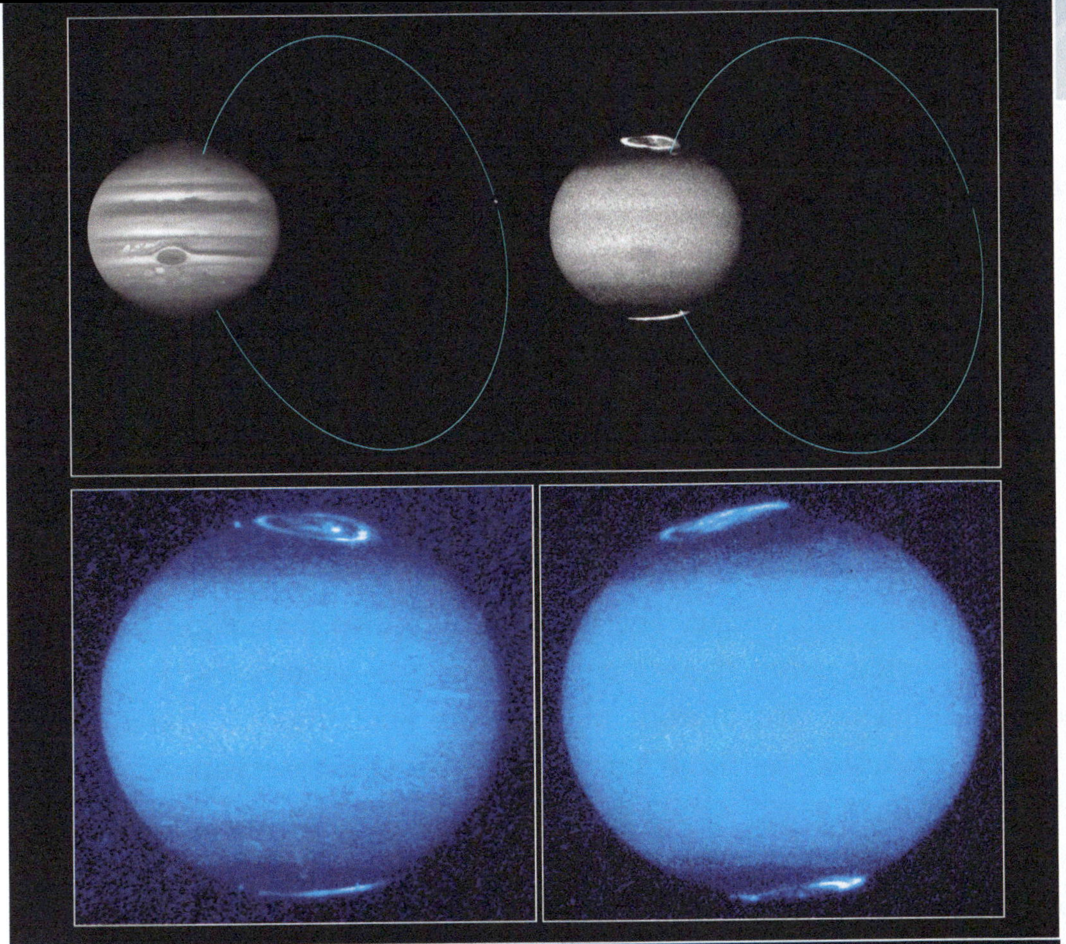

Jupiter's auroral arcs. In the top images, the path of the current of charged particles that links Jupiter and its moon Io is traced. In the top left image, Io appears as a faint dot.

THE INSIDE OF JUPITER

The atmosphere of Jupiter constitutes only a very small fraction of the planet, much as the skin of an apple compares with its contents. Because nothing can be directly observed below this thin outer layer, indirect conclusions are drawn from the evidence in order to determine the composition of the interior of Jupiter.

The observed quantities with which astronomers can work are the atmospheric temperature and pressure, mass, radius, shape, rate of rotation, heat balance, and perturbations of satellite orbits and spacecraft trajectories. From these can be calculated the ellipticity—or deviation from a perfect sphere—of the planet and its departure from an ellipsoidal shape. These latter quantities may also be predicted using theoretical descriptions, or models, for the internal distribution of material. Such models can then be tested by their agreement with the observations. The central temperature is estimated to be close to 25,000 K (44,500 °F, 24,700 °C), to be consistent with an internal source of heat that allows Jupiter to radiate about twice as much energy as it receives from the Sun. The central pressure is in the range of 50–100 million atmospheres (about 50–100 megabars). At such tremendous pressures hydrogen is expected to be in a metallic state.

Jupiter cannot be composed entirely of hydrogen; if it were, it would have to be considerably larger than it is to account for its mass. On the other hand, hydrogen must predominate, constituting at least 70 percent of the planet by mass, regardless of form—gas, liquid, or solid. The Galileo probe measured a proportion for helium of 24 percent by mass in Jupiter's upper atmosphere, compared with the

28 percent predicted if the atmosphere had the same composition as the original solar nebula. Because the planet as a whole should have that original composition, astronomers have concluded that some helium that was dissolved in the fluid hydrogen in the planet's interior has precipitated out of solution and sunk toward the planet's centre, leaving the atmosphere depleted of this gas. Evidently it has taken much of the neon with it. This precipitation is persisting as the planet continues to cool down.

Current models agree on a transition from molecular to metallic hydrogen at approximately one-fourth of the distance down toward Jupiter's centre. It should be stressed that this is not a transition between a liquid and a solid but rather between two fluids with different electrical properties. In the metallic state the electrons are no longer bound to their nuclei, thus giving hydrogen the conductivity of a metal. No solid surface exists in any of these models, although most (but not all) models incorporate a dense core with a radius of 0.03–0.1 that of Jupiter (0.33–1.1 the radius of Earth).

The source of internal heat has not been completely resolved. The currently favoured explanation invokes a combination of the gradual release of primordial heat left from the planet's formation and the liberation of thermal energy from the precipitation of droplets of helium in the planet's deep interior, as is also known to occur on

Saturn. The lower helium abundance in Jupiter's atmosphere relative to the Sun supports this latter deduction. The first process is simply the cooling phase of the original "collapse" that converted potential energy to thermal energy at the time when the planet accumulated its complement of solar nebula gas.

JUPITER'S MOONS AND RING OF JUPITER

The first objects in the solar system discovered by means of a telescope—by Galileo in 1610—were the four brightest moons of Jupiter, now called the Galilean satellites. The fifth known Jovian moon, Amalthea, was also discovered by visual observation—by Edward Emerson Barnard in 1892. All the other known satellites were found in photographs or electronic images taken with Earth-based telescopes or by the cameras on the Voyager spacecraft. Jupiter's multicomponent ring was detected in Voyager images in 1979.

Roman numerals are assigned to the first 60 known moons in order of their discovery. The orbits of the inner eight moons have low eccentricities and low inclinations; i.e., the orbits are all nearly circular and in the plane of the planet's equator. Such moons are called "regular." The orbits of the dozens of moons found beyond Callisto have much higher inclinations and eccentricities, making them "irregular." The two innermost moons, Metis and Adrastea, are intimately associated with Jupiter's ring system, as sources of the fine particles and as gravitationally controlling "shepherds." Amalthea and Thebe also contribute to the ring system by producing very tenuous gossamer rings slightly farther from the planet. There may well be additional, undiscovered small moons close to Jupiter. There almost certainly are more distant irregular moons than those so far detected.

THE GALILEAN SATELLITES

Galileo proposed that the four Jovian moons he discovered in 1610 be named the Medicean stars, in honour of his patron, Cosimo II de' Medici, but they soon came to be known as the Galilean satellites in honour of their discoverer. Galileo regarded their existence as a fundamental argument in favour of the Copernican model of the solar system, in which the planets orbit the Sun. Their orbits around Jupiter were in flagrant violation of the Ptolemaic system, in which all celestial objects must move around Earth.

In order of increasing distance from the planet, these satellites are called Io, Europa, Ganymede, and Callisto, for figures closely associated with Jupiter in Greek mythology.

Although approximate diameters and spectroscopic characteristics of the Galilean moons had been determined from Earth-based observations, it was the Voyager missions that indelibly established these four bodies as worlds in their own right. The Galileo mission provided a wealth of additional data. Before Voyager it was known that Callisto and Ganymede are both as large as or larger than the planet Mercury; that they and Europa have surfaces covered with water ice; that Io's orbit is surrounded by a torus of atoms and ions that include sodium, potassium, and sulfur; and that the inner two Galilean moons have mean densities much greater than those of the outer two. This density gradient from Io to Callisto resembles that found in the solar system itself and seems to result from the same cause. The density values suggest that Io and Europa have a rocky composition similar to that of the Moon, whereas roughly 50 percent of Ganymede and Callisto must be made of a much less dense substance, water ice being the obvious candidate.

CALLISTO

The icy surface of this satellite is so dominated by impact craters that there are no smooth plains like the dark maria observed on the Moon. In other words, there seem to be no areas on Callisto where upwelling of material from subsequent internal activity has obliterated any of the record of early bombardment. This record was formed by impacting debris (comet nuclei and asteroidal material) primarily during the first 500 million years after the formation of the solar system in much the same way that the craters on the Moon were produced. The unmodified appearance of the surface is consistent with the absence of a differentiated interior. Evidently no tidally induced global heating and consequent melting occurred on Callisto, unlike the other three Galilean moons. The Galileo spacecraft revealed that craters smaller than 10 km (6 miles) are hidden by drifts of fine, dark material resembling a mixture of clay minerals.

In addition to the predominant water ice, solid carbon dioxide is present on the surface, and an extremely tenuous carbon dioxide atmosphere is slowly escaping into space. Other trace surface constituents are hydrogen peroxide, probably produced from the ice by photochemical reactions driven by solar ultraviolet radiation; sulfur and sulfur compounds, probably coming from Io; and organic compounds that may have been delivered by cometary impacts. Callisto has a weak magnetic field induced by Jupiter's field that may imply the existence of a layer of liquid water below its icy crust.

GANYMEDE

Unlike Callisto, Ganymede, an equally icy satellite, reveals distinct patches of dark and light terrain. This contrast is reminiscent of the Moon's surface, but the answer to which terrain came first—dark or light—is exactly reversed. In contrast to the Moon, the dark regions on Ganymede are

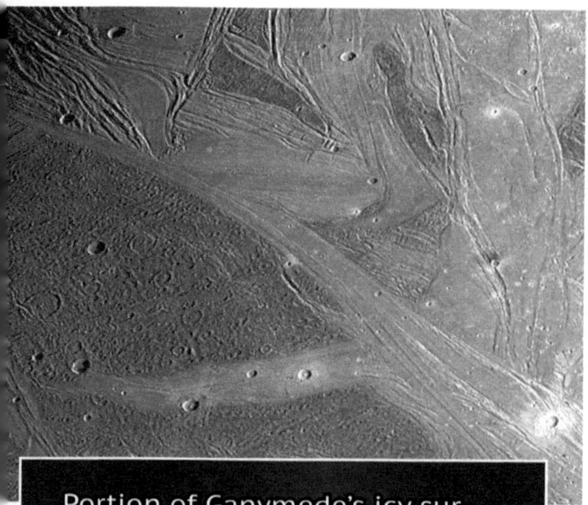

Portion of Ganymede's icy surface showing characteristic dark and light grooved terrain, as recorded by the Galileo spacecraft on May 7, 1997.

the older areas, showing the heaviest concentration of craters. The light regions are younger, revealing a complex pattern of parallel and intersecting ridges and grooves in addition to unusually bright impact craters typically surrounded by systems of rays.

This manifestation of active crustal movement and resurfacing is accompanied by clear evidence of internal differentiation. Unlike Callisto, Ganymede has an iron-rich core and a permanent magnetic field that is strong enough to create its own magnetosphere and auroras. Hubble Space Telescope observations of how Ganymede's auroras change when interacting with Jupiter's magnetic field reveal the likely existence of a subsurface ocean about 100 km (60 miles) thick. The trace components identified in Ganymede's icy surface include a smaller amount of the same claylike dust found on Callisto and the same traces of solid carbon dioxide, hydrogen peroxide, and sulfur compounds, plus evidence for molecular oxygen and ozone trapped in the ice.

EUROPA

The surface of Europa is totally different from that of Ganymede or Callisto, despite the fact that the infrared spectrum of this object indicates that it, too, is covered with ice. There are few impact craters on Europa—the number per unit area is comparable to that on the continental regions of Earth, indicating that the surface is relatively recent. Some scientists think the surface is so young that significant resurfacing is still taking place on the satellite. This resurfacing evidently consists of the outflow of water from the interior to form an instant frozen ocean.

Models for the differentiated interior suggest the presence of an iron-rich core surrounded by a silicate mantle surmounted by an icy crust some 150 km (90 miles) thick. This moon possesses both induced and intrinsic magnetic fields. Slightly mottled regions on the surface have been found to contain salt deposits, suggesting evaporation of water from a reservoir below the crust. Europa's frozen surface is crisscrossed with dark and bright stripes and curvilinear ridges and grooves. Spatter cones along some of the grooves again suggest fluid eruptions from below. The relief is extremely low, with ridge heights perhaps a few hundred metres at most. Europa thus has the smoothest surface of any solid body examined in the solar system thus far. Traces of sulfur, sulfur compounds, hydrogen peroxide, and

An elaborately patterned area of disrupted ice crust on Europa's surface, which indicates that its crust cracked and huge blocks of ice rotated slightly before being refrozen in new positions.

organic compounds have been identified on the surface.

The major open question is whether a global ocean of liquid water is beneath Europa's ice, warmed by the release of tidal energy in Europa's interior. The possibility of such an ocean arose from Voyager data, and high-resolution Galileo images suggested fluid activity near the surface. In addition, explanation of Europa's induced magnetic field appears to require an interior, electrically conducting fluid medium, implying a salt-containing liquid water layer at some depth beneath the surface ice. If this ocean and its required source of heat exist, the possible presence of at least microbial life-forms may be likely.

IO

Seen through a telescope from Earth, Io appears reddish orange, while the other moons are neutral in tint. Io's infrared spectrum shows no evidence of the absorption characteristics of water ice. Scientists expected Io's surface to look different from those of Jupiter's other moons, but the Voyager images revealed a landscape even more unusual than anticipated.

Volcanic fissures, instead of impact craters, dot the surface of Io. Nine volcanoes were observed in eruption when the two Voyager spacecraft flew by in 1979, while the closer encounters by Galileo indicated that as many as 300 volcanic vents may be active at a given time. The silicate lava emerging from the vents is extremely hot (about 1,900 K [3,000 °F, 1,630 °C]), resembling primitive lavas on early Earth. This unprecedented level of activity makes Io the most tectonically active object in the solar system.

The surface of the satellite is continually and completely replaced by this volcanism in just a few thousand years. Various forms (allotropes) of sulfur appear to be responsible for the black, orange, and red areas on the moon's surface, while solid sulfur dioxide is probably the main constituent of the white areas. Sulfur dioxide was detected as a gas near one of the active volcanic plumes by Voyager's infrared spectrometer and was identified as a solid in ultraviolet and infrared spectra obtained from Earth-orbital and ground-based observations.

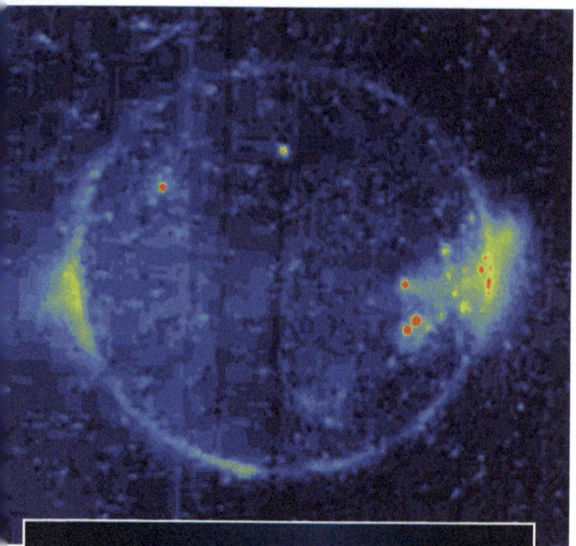

Colour-enhanced image of Io. Red and yellow-green spots are probably lava flows or lakes, while the bright area extending from Io's left limb corresponds to a volcano plume.

These identifications provide sources for the sulfur and oxygen ions observed in the Jovian magnetosphere and prove that Io's volcanic activity is the source of its torus of particles.

The energy for this volcanic activity requires a special explanation, since radioactive heating is inadequate for a body as small as Io. The favoured explanation is based on the observation that orbital resonances with the other Galilean satellites perturb Io into a more eccentric orbit than it would assume if only Jupiter controlled its motion. The resulting tides developed by the gravitational contest over Io between the other satellites and Jupiter release enough energy to account for the observed volcanism. The interior contains a dense, iron-rich core, which probably produces a magnetic field. The interactions of Io with Jupiter's magnetosphere and ionosphere are so complex, however, that it has been difficult to distinguish the satellite's own field from the current-produced fields in its vicinity.

JUPITER'S OTHER SATELLITES

The only other Jovian moon that was close enough to the trajectories of the Voyager spacecraft to allow surface features to be seen was Amalthea. So small that its gravitational field is not strong enough to deform it into a sphere, it has an irregular, oblong shape. Like Io, its surface exhibits a reddish colour that may result from a coating of sulfur compounds released by Io's volcanoes.

In addition to providing new images of Amalthea, the Galileo orbiter was able to view the effect of impacts on Thebe and Metis. All three of these inner moons are tidally locked, keeping the same face oriented toward Jupiter. All three are some 30 percent brighter on their leading sides, presumably as a result of impacts by small meteoroids. Amalthea has a remarkably low density, implying a highly porous structure that probably resulted from internal shattering by impacts.

Before the turn of the 21st century, eight outer moons were known, comprising two distinct orbital families. The more distant group—made up of Ananke, Carme, Pasiphae, and Sinope— has retrograde orbits around Jupiter. The closer group—Leda, Himalia, Lysithea, and Elara—has prograde orbits. (In the case of these moons, retrograde motion is in the direction opposite to Jupiter's spin and motion around the Sun, which are counterclockwise as viewed from above Jupiter's north pole, whereas prograde, or direct, motion is in the same direction.)

In 1999 astronomers began a concerted effort to find new Jovian satellites using highly sensitive electronic detectors that allowed them to detect fainter—and hence smaller—objects. When in the next few years they discovered a host of additional outer moons, they recognized that the two-family division was an oversimplification. There must be well more than 100 small fragments orbiting Jupiter that can be classified into several different groups according to their orbits. Each group apparently originated from an individual body that was captured by Jupiter and then broke up. The captures could have occurred near the time of Jupiter's formation when the planet was itself surrounded by a nebula that could slow down objects that entered it.

These small moons may be related to the so-called Trojan asteroids, two groups of minor planets that share Jupiter's orbit. The Trojans occupy regions 60° ahead of and behind the position of the planet in its orbit. These regions are the L4 and L5 equilibrium points in Lagrange's solution to the three-body problem.

JUPITER'S RING

As the Pioneer 10 spacecraft sped toward its closest approach to Jupiter in 1974, it detected a sudden decrease in the density of charged particles roughly 125,000 km (78,000 miles) from Jupiter, just inside the orbit of its innermost moon, Metis. This led to the suggestion that a moon or a ring of material might be orbiting the planet at this distance. The existence of a ring was verified in 1979 by the first Voyager spacecraft when it crossed the planet's equatorial plane, and the second spacecraft recorded additional pictures, including a series taken in the shadow of the planet looking back at the ring toward the direction of the Sun.

The ring was many times brighter from this perspective. Evidently most of the ring particles scatter light forward much better than in the reverse direction (toward Earth). It was therefore no surprise that Earth-based observations failed to discover the ring before Voyager. The forward scattering implies that most of the particles are very small, in the micrometre size range, rather like the motes of dust seen in a sunbeam on Earth or the fine particles on car windshield, which show the same optical effect.

The ring exhibits a complex structure that was elucidated by images obtained with the Galileo spacecraft in 1996–97. It consists of four principal components: an outer gossamer ring that fades into invisibility beyond the orbital radius of the satellite Thebe (222,000 km [138,000 miles]); an inner gossamer ring bounded by the orbit of Amalthea (181,000 km [112,000 miles]); the main ring, about 30 km

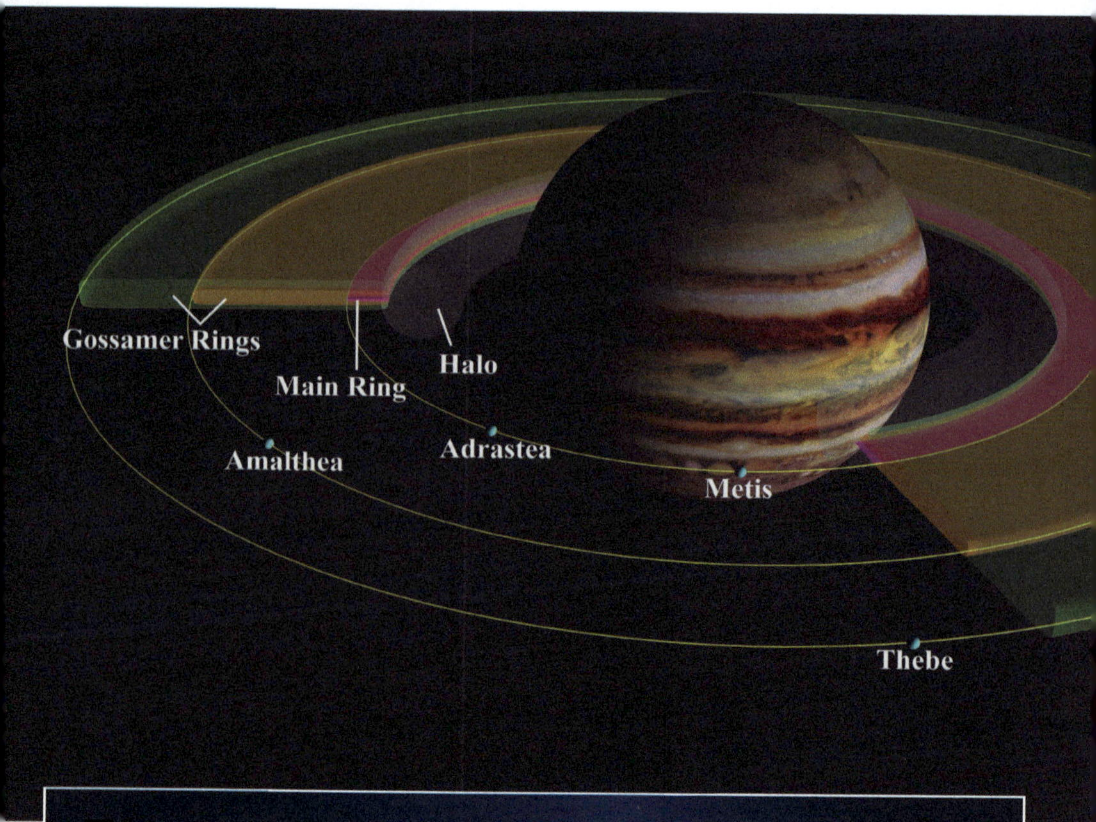

Illustration of Jupiter's ring system and small inner moons.

(20 miles) thick, which extends inward from the orbits of Adrastea (129,000 km [80,000 miles]) and Metis (128,000 km [79,500 miles]) to an inner edge at 123,000 km (76,000 miles); and a toroidal halo of particles with a thickness of 20,000 km (12,000 miles) that extends from the main ring inward to 92,000 km (57,000 miles).

The presence of micrometre-size particles in the ring requires a source, and the association of the ring boundaries with the four moons makes the source clear. The ring particles are generated by impacts on these moons (and on still smaller bodies within the main ring) by micrometeoroids, cometary debris, and possibly volcanically produced material from Io. Some of the finest particles are electrically charged and respond to the rocking motion of the Jovian magnetic field as the planet rotates.

CHAPTER 2

SATURN: THE JEWEL OF THE SOLAR SYSTEM

Saturn is the second largest planet of the solar system in mass and size and the sixth in distance from the Sun. Dusty chunks of ice—some the size of a house, others of a grain of sand—make up its extraordinary rings. The other outer planets also have rings, but Saturn's are much larger and more complex. The planet is a popular target for amateur astronomers, because even a small telescope can reveal these dazzling rings.

Saturn's name comes from the Roman god of agriculture, who is equated with the Greek deity Cronus, one of the Titans and the father of Zeus (the Roman god Jupiter). As the farthest of the planets known to ancient observers, Saturn also was noted to be the slowest-moving. At a distance from the Sun that is 9.5 times as far as Earth's, Saturn takes approximately 29.5 Earth years to make one solar revolution.

The Italian astronomer Galileo in 1610 was the first to observe Saturn with a telescope. Although he saw a

Saturn and its rings. Shadows cast by the rings are visible against the bluish northern hemisphere, while the planet's shadow is projected on the rings to the left.

strangeness in Saturn's appearance, the low resolution of his instrument did not allow him to discern the true nature of the planet's rings.

Saturn occupies almost 60 percent of Jupiter's volume but has only about one-third of its mass and the lowest mean density—about 70 percent that of water—of any known object in the solar system. Hypothetically, Saturn would float in an ocean large enough to hold it.

Both Saturn and Jupiter resemble stars in that their bulk chemical composition is dominated by hydrogen. Also, as is the case for Jupiter, the tremendous pressure in Saturn's deep interior maintains the hydrogen there in a fluid metallic state. Saturn's structure and evolutionary history, however, differ significantly from those of its larger counterpart.

Like the other Jovian, planets, Saturn has extensive systems of moons (natural satellites) and rings, which may provide clues to its origin and evolution as well as to those of the solar system. Saturn's moon Titan is distinguished from all other moons in the solar system by the presence of a significant atmosphere, one that is denser than that of any of the terrestrial planets except Venus.

The greatest advances in knowledge of Saturn, as well as of most of the other planets, have come from deep-space probes. Four spacecraft have visited the Saturnian system: Pioneer 11 in 1979, Voyagers 1 and 2 in the two years following, and, after almost a quarter-century, Cassini-Huygens, which arrived in 2004. The first three missions were short-term flybys, but Cassini went into orbit around Saturn for years of investigations, while its Huygens probe parachuted through the atmosphere of Titan and reached its surface, becoming the first spacecraft to land on a moon other than Earth's.

AN OVERVIEW OF SATURN

Saturn orbits the Sun at a mean distance of 1,427,000,000 km (887 million miles). Its closest distance to Earth is about 1.2 billion km (746 million miles), and its phase angle—the angle that it makes with the Sun and Earth—never exceeds about 6°. Saturn seen from the vicinity of Earth thus always appears nearly fully illuminated. Only deep space probes can provide sidelit and backlit views.

Like Jupiter and most of the other planets, Saturn has a regular orbit—that is, its motion around the Sun is prograde (in the same direction that the Sun rotates) and has a small eccentricity (noncircularity) and inclination to the ecliptic, the plane of Earth's orbit. Unlike Jupiter, however, Saturn's rotational axis is tilted substantially—by 26.7°—to its orbital plane. The tilt gives Saturn seasons, as on Earth, but each season lasts more than seven years.

Saturn's rotation period has not yet been well determined. Cloud motions in its massive upper atmosphere trace out a variety of periods, which are as short as about 10 hours 10 minutes near the equator and increase with some oscillation to about 30 minutes longer at latitudes higher than 40°. Scientists have attempted to determine the rotation period of Saturn's deep interior from that of its magnetic field, which is presumed to be rooted in the planet's metallic-hydrogen outer core. Direct measurement of the field's rotation is difficult because the field is highly symmetrical around the rotational axis.

At the time of the Voyager encounters, radio outbursts from Saturn, apparently related to small irregularities in the magnetic field, showed a period of 10 hours 39.4 minutes; this value was taken to be the magnetic field rotation period. Measurements made 25 years later by the Cassini spacecraft indicated that the field was rotating with a period 6 to 7 minutes longer. It is believed that the solar wind is responsible for some of the difference between the two measurements of the rotational period. Other analyses based on Saturn's shape and interior structure suggested that the internal rotation period could be as short as 10 hours 32 minutes or as long as 10 hours 41 minutes. The time differences between the rotation periods of Saturn's clouds and of its interior have been used to estimate wind velocities.

Because the four giant planets have no solid surface in their outer layers, by convention the values for the radius and gravity of these planets are calculated at the level at which one bar of atmospheric pressure is exerted. By this measure, Saturn's equatorial diameter is 120,536 km (74,898 miles). In comparison, its polar diameter is only 108,728 km (67,560 miles), or 10 percent smaller, which makes Saturn the most oblate (flattened at the poles) of all the planets in the solar system. Its oblate shape is apparent even in a small telescope. Even though Saturn rotates slightly slower than Jupiter, it is more oblate because its rotational acceleration cancels a larger fraction of the planet's gravity at the equator. The equatorial gravity of the planet, 896 cm (29.4 feet) per second per second, is only 74 percent of its polar gravity.

Saturn is 95 times as massive as Earth but occupies a volume 766 times greater. Its mean density of 0.69 gram per cubic cm is thus only some 12 percent of Earth's. Saturn's equatorial escape velocity—the velocity needed for an object, which includes individual atoms and molecules, to escape the planet's gravitational attraction at the equator without having to be further accelerated—is nearly 36 km per second (80,000 miles per hour) at the one-bar level, compared with 11.2 km per second (25,000 miles per hour) for Earth. This high value indicates that there has been no significant loss of atmosphere from Saturn since its formation.

Saturn, showing an Earth-sized storm (light-coloured patch) in its northern equatorial region.

COMPOSITION AND STRUCTURE OF SATURN'S ATMOSPHERE

Viewed from Earth, Saturn has an overall hazy yellow-brown appearance. The surface that is seen through telescopes and in spacecraft images is actually a complex of cloud layers decorated by many small-scale features, such as red, brown, and white spots, bands, eddies, and vortices, that vary over a fairly short time. In this way Saturn resembles a blander and less active Jupiter. A spectacular exception occurred during September–November 1990, when a large, light-coloured storm system appeared near the equator, expanded to a size exceeding 20,000 km (12,400 miles), and eventually spread around the equator before fading. Storms similar in impressiveness to this "Great White Spot" (so named in analogy with Jupiter's Great Red Spot) have been observed at about 30-year intervals dating back to the late 19th century. This is close to Saturn's orbital period of 29.4 years, which suggests that these storms are seasonal phenomena.

Saturn's atmosphere is composed mostly of molecular hydrogen and helium. The exact relative abundance of the two molecules is not well known, since helium must be measured indirectly. Currently the best estimate is that the planet's atmosphere is 18 to 25 percent helium by mass. The remainder is molecular hydrogen and about 2 percent other molecules. Helium is less abundant relative to hydrogen compared with the composition of the Sun. If hydrogen, helium, and other elements were present in the same proportions as in the Sun's atmosphere, Saturn's atmosphere would be about 71 percent hydrogen and 28 percent helium by mass. According to some theories, helium may have settled out of Saturn's outer layers.

Other major molecules observed in Saturn's atmosphere are methane and ammonia, which are two to seven times more abundant relative to hydrogen than in the Sun. Hydrogen sulfide and water are also suspected to be present in the deeper atmosphere but have not yet been detected. Minor molecules that have been detected spectroscopically from Earth include phosphine, carbon monoxide, and germane. Such molecules would not be present in detectable amounts in a hydrogen-rich atmosphere in chemical equilibrium. They may be products of reactions at high pressure and temperature in Saturn's deep atmosphere, well below the observable clouds, that have been transported to visible atmospheric regions by convective motions.

A number of other nonequilibrium hydrocarbons are observed in Saturn's stratosphere: acetylene, ethane, and, possibly, propane and methyl acetylene. All of the latter may be produced by photochemical effects from solar ultraviolet radiation or, at higher latitudes, by energetic electrons precipitating from Saturn's radiation belts.

Astronomers on Earth have analyzed the refraction (bending) of starlight and radio waves from spacecraft passing through Saturn's atmosphere to gain information on atmospheric temperature over depths corresponding to pressures of one-millionth of a bar to 1.3 bars. At pressures less than 1 millibar, the temperature is roughly constant at about 140 to 150 kelvins (K; −208 to −190 °F, −133 to −123 °C). A stratosphere, where temperatures steadily decline with increasing pressure, extends downward from 1 to 60 millibars, at which level the coldest temperature in Saturn's atmosphere, 82 K (−312 °F, −191 °C), is reached. At higher pressures (deeper levels) the temperature increases once again. This region is analogous to the lowest layer of Earth's atmosphere, the troposphere, in which the increase of temperature with pressure follows the thermodynamic relation for compression of a gas without gain or loss of heat. The temperature is 135 K (−217 °F, −138 °C) at a pressure of 1 bar, and it continues to increase at higher pressures.

Saturn's visible layer of clouds is formed from molecules of minor compounds that condense in the hydrogen-rich atmosphere. Although particles formed from photochemical reactions are seen suspended high in the atmosphere at levels corresponding to pressures of 20–70 millibars, the main clouds commence at a level where the pressure exceeds 400 millibars, with the highest cloud deck thought to be formed of solid ammonia crystals.

A consequence of Saturn's large axial tilt is that the rings cast dark shadows onto the winter hemisphere, further reducing the dim winter sunlight. Cassini images of sunlit swaths of the northern hemisphere during winter revealed a surprisingly clear blue atmosphere, which perhaps was a consequence of the comparative lack of photochemical haze production in the shadows of the rings.

A DYNAMIC ATMOSPHERE

Like the other giant planets, Saturn has an atmospheric circulation that is dominated by zonal (east-west) flow. This manifests itself as a pattern of lighter and darker cloud bands similar to Jupiter's, although Saturn's bands are more subtly coloured and are wider near the equator. The features in the cloud tops have such low contrast that they are best studied by spacecraft.

Since Saturn lacks a surface, its winds must be measured relative to some other frame of reference. As with Jupiter, the winds are measured with respect to the rotation of Saturn's magnetic field. In this frame, virtually all of Saturn's atmospheric flows are to the east—in the direction of rotation. The equatorial zone at latitudes below 20° shows a particularly active eastward flow having a maximum velocity close to 470 metres per second (1,700 km [1,050 miles] per hour) but with periods when the velocity is 200 metres per second (700 km [450 miles] per hour) slower. This feature is analogous to one on Jupiter but extends twice as wide in latitude and moves four times faster. By contrast, the highest winds on Earth occur in tropical cyclones, where in extreme cases sustained velocities may exceed 67 metres per second (240 km [150 miles] per hour).

Unlike hurricanes on Earth, there is no ocean below Saturn's vortices. The first jet to the south of the northern vortex at 75° N follows a hexagonal pattern around the planet. Cloud features are observed to move around the hexagon counterclockwise at about 100 metres per second (360 km [220 miles] per hour). Similar angular patterns have been observed in buckets of spinning fluids and probably arise from interacting waves. Why the hexagonal wave is stable and how it developed at this particular latitude in Saturn's atmosphere is not yet understood.

A rich variety of smaller-scale features has also been observed in the atmosphere. Particularly striking are about two dozen similarly sized (1,500 km [930 miles] in diameter) cloud clearings spaced nearly uniformly across 100° of longitude near 33.5° N. In infrared images of Saturn's thermal emission these clearings appear as a bright "string of pearls" stretching across the planet. In the southern hemisphere, shortwave radio emissions from lightning storms, hundreds of times more intense than those on Earth and lasting weeks to months, were frequently detected by Cassini at 35° S. The thunderstorm centres are associated with thick light-coloured cloud features apparently produced by strong convective motions driven by water vapour. Both the latitudes of the cloud clearings in the north and the lightning storms in the south are zones of fast westward winds, traveling opposite to most of the other zonal flows on the planet.

The general north-south symmetry suggests that the zonal flows may be connected in some fashion deep within the interior. Theoretical modeling of a deep-convecting fluid planet such as Saturn indicates that differential rotation tends to occur along cylinders aligned about the planet's mean rotation axis. Saturn's atmosphere thus may be built of a series of coaxial cylinders aligned north-south, each rotating at a unique rate, which give rise to the zonal jets seen at the surface. The continuity of the cylinders may be broken at a point where they intersect a major discontinuity within Saturn, such as the core.

THE MAGNETIC FIELD AND MAGNETOSPHERE

Saturn's magnetic field resembles that of a simple dipole, or bar magnet, its north-south axis aligned to within 1° of Saturn's rotation axis with the centre of the magnetic dipole at the centre of the planet. The polarity of the field, like Jupiter's, is opposite that of Earth's present field—i.e., the field lines emerge in Saturn's northern hemisphere and reenter the planet in the southern hemisphere. On Saturn a common magnetic compass would point south.

Saturn's magnetic field is generated by the fluid motions in the electrically conducting portion of the interior of the planet. This region, in which hydrogen exists in a fluid metallic state around a central rocky core, comprises the inner half of the planet. Compared with Jupiter, less of Saturn's mass and volume consists of this conducting metallic fluid, which may partly explain why Saturn's magnetic field is much weaker. Jupiter's interior is also hotter, so the fluid motions in its interior may be more vigorous, possibly contributing even further to the differences in the field strengths.

Saturn's magnetosphere is the teardrop-shaped region of space around the planet where the behaviour of charged particles, which come mostly from the Sun, is dominated by the planet's magnetic field rather than by interplanetary magnetic fields. The rounded side of the teardrop extends sunward, forming a boundary, or magnetopause, with the outflowing solar wind at a distance of about 20 Saturn radii (1,200,000 km [750,000 miles]) from the centre of the planet but with substantial fluctuation due to variations in the pressure from the solar wind. On the opposite side of Saturn, the magnetosphere is drawn out into an immense magnetotail that extends to great distances.

Saturn's inner magnetosphere, like the magnetospheres of Earth and Jupiter, traps a stable population of highly energetic charged particles, mostly protons, traveling in spiral paths along magnetic field lines. These particles form belts around Saturn similar to the Van Allen belts of Earth. Unlike the cases of Earth and Jupiter, Saturn's charged-particle population is substantially depleted by absorption of the particles onto the surfaces of solid bodies that orbit within the field lines. Voyager data showed that "holes" exist in the particle populations on field lines that intersect the rings and the orbits of moons within the magnetosphere.

Saturn possesses ultraviolet auroras produced by the impact of energetic particles from the magnetosphere onto atomic and molecular hydrogen in Saturn's polar atmosphere. Ultraviolet images of Saturn taken by the Earth-orbiting Hubble Space Telescope in the late 1990s and early 21st century succeeded in capturing the auroral rings around the poles. These gave vivid evidence of the high symmetry of Saturn's magnetic field and revealed details of the way the auroras respond to the solar wind and the Sun's magnetic field.

SATURN'S INTERIOR

Saturn's low mean density is direct evidence that its bulk composition is mostly hydrogen. Under the conditions found within the planet, hydrogen behaves as a liquid rather than a gas at pressures above about one kilobar, corresponding to a depth of 1,000 km (600 miles) below the clouds; there the temperature is roughly 1,000 K (1,340 °F, 730 °C). Even as a liquid, molecular hydrogen is a highly compressible material, and to achieve Saturn's mean density of 0.69 gram per cubic cm requires pressures above one megabar. This occurs at a depth of 20,000 km (12,500 miles) below the clouds, or about one-third of the distance to the planet's centre.

Analysis shows that Saturn is substantially more centrally condensed than Jupiter and therefore contains a significantly larger amount of material denser than hydrogen near its centre. Saturn's central regions contain about 50 percent hydrogen by mass, while Jupiter's contain approximately 67 percent hydrogen. At a pressure of roughly two megabars and a temperature of about 6,000 K (10,300 °F, 5,730 °C), the fluid molecular hydrogen is predicted to undergo a major phase transition to a fluid metallic state, which resembles a molten alkali metal such as lithium. This transition occurs at a distance about halfway between Saturn's cloud tops and its centre. Evidence from the planet's gravitational field shows that the central metallic region is considerably denser than would be the case for pure hydrogen mixed only with solar proportions of helium. Excess helium that settled from the planet's outer layers might account partly for the increased density. In addition, Saturn may contain a quantity of material denser than both hydrogen and helium with a total mass as much as 30 times that of Earth, but its precise distribution cannot be determined from available data. A rock and ice mixture of about 10–20 Earth masses is likely to be concentrated in a dense central core.

The calculated electrical conductivity of Saturn's outer core of fluid metallic hydrogen is such that if slow circulation currents are present—as would be expected with the flow of heat to the surface accompanied by gravitational settling of denser components—there is sufficient dynamo action to generate the planet's observed magnetic field. Saturn's field thus is produced by essentially the same mechanism that produces Earth's field.

On average, Saturn radiates about twice as much energy into space than it receives from the Sun, primarily at infrared wavelengths between 20 and 100 micrometres. This difference indicates that Saturn, like Jupiter, possesses a source of internal heat. Kilogram for kilogram of mass, Saturn's internal energy output at present is similar to Jupiter's. But Saturn is less massive than Jupiter and so had less total energy content at the time both planets were formed. For it still to be radiating at Jupiter's level means that its energy apparently is coming at least partially from a different source.

A calculation of thermal evolution shows that Saturn could have originated with a core of 10–20 Earth masses built up from the accretion of ice-rich planetesimals. On top of this, a large amount of gaseous hydrogen and helium from the original solar nebula would have accumulated by gravitational collapse. It is thought that Jupiter underwent a similar process of origin but that it captured an even greater amount of gas.

On both planets the gas was heated to high temperatures—several tens of thousands of kelvins—in the course of the capture. Jupiter's present internal energy output can then be understood as the slow cooling of an initially hot planet over the age of the solar system, some 4.6 billion years. If Saturn had slowly cooled, its energy output would have dropped below the presently observed value about two billion years ago.

The most likely explanation for the required additional energy source is that in Saturn's interior helium has been precipitating from solution in hydrogen and forming dense "raindrops" that fall. As the helium droplets in the metallic phase of hydrogen "rain" down into deeper levels, potential energy is converted into the kinetic energy of droplet motion. Friction then damps this motion and converts it into heat, which is carried up to the atmosphere by convection and radiated into space, thus prolonging Saturn's internal heat source. The Voyagers' detection of a substantial depletion of helium in Saturn's atmosphere originally was taken as a vindication of this theory, but it has since been opened to question.

SATURN'S COMPLEX RING SYSTEM

Although Saturn's rings and moons may seem to constitute two groups of quite different entities, they form a single complex system of objects whose structures, dynamics, and evolution are intimately linked. The orbits of the innermost known moons fall within or between the outermost rings, and new moons continue to be found embedded in the ring structure. Indeed, the ring system itself can be considered to consist of myriad tiny moons—ranging from mere dust specks to car- and house-sized pieces—in their own individual orbits around Saturn. Because of the difficulty in distinguishing between the largest ring particles and the smallest moons, determining a precise number of moons for Saturn may not be possible.

Like the rings of the other giant planets, Saturn's major rings lie within the classical Roche limit. This distance, which for the idealized case is 2.44 Saturn radii

Discovering Saturn's Rings

In 1610, Galileo's first observations of Saturn with a primitive telescope prompted him to report: "Saturn is not a single star, but is a composite of three, which almost touch each other, never change or move relative to each other, and are arranged in a row along the zodiac, the middle one being three times larger than the lateral ones."

Two years later he was perplexed to find that the image in his telescope had become a single object; Earth had crossed Saturn's ring plane, and, viewed edge on, the rings had essentially disappeared. Later observations showed Galileo that the curious lateral appendages had returned. Apparently he never deduced that the appendages were in fact a disk encircling the planet.

The Dutch scientist Christiaan Huygens, who began studying Saturn with an improved telescope in 1655, eventually deduced the true shape of the rings and the fact that the ring plane was inclined substantially to Saturn's orbit. He believed, however, that the rings were a single solid disk with a substantial thickness.

In 1675 the Italian-born French astronomer Gian Domenico Cassini's discovery of a large gap—now

Image of Saturn captured by Cassini during the first radio occultation observation of the planet, which situated Cassini and Earth on opposite sides of Saturn's rings.

known as the Cassini division—within the disk cast doubt on the possibility of a solid ring, and the French mathematician and scientist Pierre-Simon Laplace published a theory in 1789 that the rings were made up of many smaller components. In 1857 the Scottish physicist James Clerk Maxwell demonstrated mathematically that the rings could be stable only if they comprised a very large number of small particles, a deduction confirmed about 40 years later by the American astronomer James Keeler.

(CONTINUED ON THE NEXT PAGE)

(CONTINUED FROM THE PREVIOUS PAGE)

Today it is known that, while Saturn's rings are enormous, they are also extremely thin. The major rings have a diameter of 270,000 km (170,000 miles), yet their thickness does not exceed 100 metres (330 feet), and their total mass comprises only about 3×10^{19} kg, about the mass of Saturn's moon Mimas. The entire ring system spans nearly 26,000,000 km (16,000,000 miles) when the faint outer rings are included.

(147,000 km [91,300 miles]), represents the closest distance to which a fairly large moon can approach the centre of its more-massive planetary parent before it is torn apart by tidal forces. Conversely, small bodies within the Roche limit are prevented by tidal forces from aggregating into larger objects. The limit applies only to objects held together by gravitational attraction; it does not restrict the stability of a relatively small body for which molecular cohesion is more important than the tidal forces tending to pull it apart. Thus, small moons (and artificial satellites) with sizes in the range of tens of kilometres or less can persist indefinitely within the Roche limit.

Although the individual particles that make up Saturn's rings cannot be seen directly, their size distribution can be deduced from their effect on the scattering of light and radio signals propagated through the rings from stars and spacecraft. This analysis reveals a broad and continuous spectrum of particle sizes, ranging from centimetres to several metres, with larger objects being significantly fewer in number than smaller ones.

This distribution is consistent with the result expected from repeated collision and shattering of initially larger objects. In some parts of the rings, where collisions are apparently more frequent, even smaller (dust-sized) grains are present, but these have short lifetimes owing to a variety of loss mechanisms. Clouds of the smaller grains apparently acquire electric charges, interact with Saturn's magnetic field, and manifest themselves in the form of moving, wedge-shaped spokes that extend radially over the plane of the rings.

The rings strongly reflect sunlight, and a spectroscopic analysis of the reflected light shows the presence of water ice, in addition to darker contaminants. It is thus conceivable that the major rings were produced by the breakup of a moon the size and composition of Titan. The outer icy layer of the moon was stripped off to become the rings, while the inner rocky core of the moon fell into Saturn. The new ring system would have been much larger than the rings today and would have shrunk by forming the icy inner moons such as Tethys.

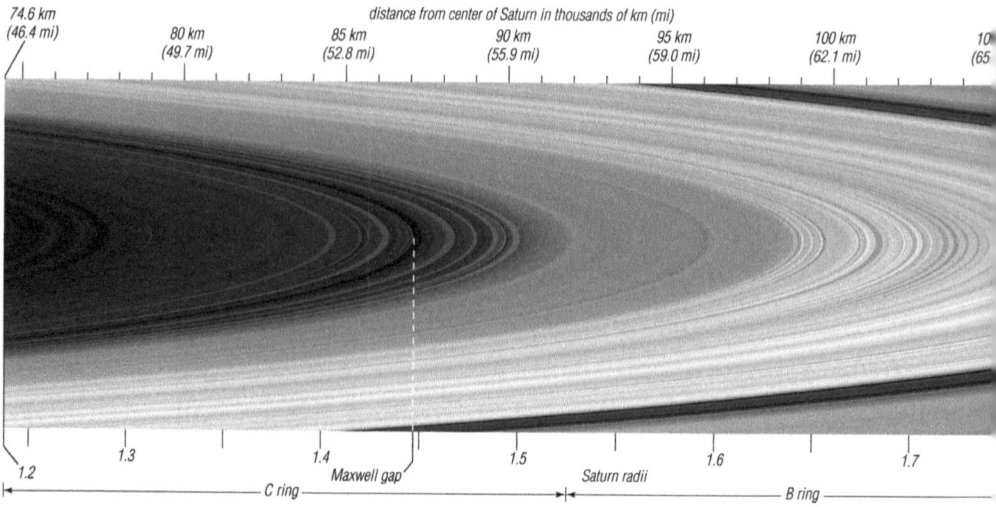

Details of Saturn's three main rings, in a natural-colour composite of six images obtained by the Cassini spacecraft on December 12, 2004.

The main ring system shows structures on many scales, ranging from the three broad major rings—named C, B, and A (in order of increasing distance from Saturn)—that are visible from Earth down to myriad individual component ringlets having widths on the order of kilometres. The structures have provided scientists a fertile field for investigating gravitational resonances and the collective effects of many small particles orbiting in close proximity. Although many of the structures have been explained theoretically, a large number remain enigmatic, and a complete synthesis of the system is still lacking. Because Saturn's ring system

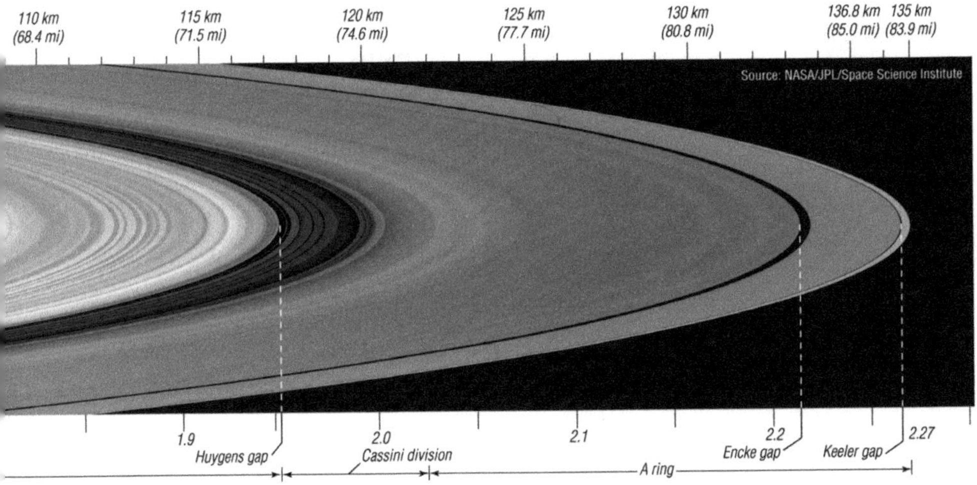

may be an analogue of the original disk-shaped system of particles out of which the planets formed, an understanding of its dynamics and evolution has implications for the origin of the solar system itself.

SATURN'S MOONS

Saturn possesses more than 60 known moons. All of the inner moons are regular, having prograde, low-inclination, and low-eccentricity orbits with respect to the planet. The eight largest are thought to have formed along Saturn's equatorial plane from a protoplanetary disk of material, in much the same way as the planets formed around the

Hubble Space Telescope image of Saturn and several of its moons. At the north pole, the shadow of Titan is visible; below it is Mimas. Dione and Enceladus are faintly visible at left.

Sun from the primordial solar nebula.

A second, outer group of moons lies beyond about 11 million km (6.8 million miles). They are irregular in that all of their orbits have large eccentricities and inclinations; about two-thirds revolve around Saturn in a retrograde fashion—they move opposite to the planet's rotation. Except for Phoebe, they are less than about 20 km (12 miles) in radius.

Some were discovered from Earth beginning in 2000 as the result of efforts to apply new electronic detection methods to the search for fainter—and hence smaller—objects in the solar system; others were found by Cassini. These outer bodies appear to be not primordial moons but rather captured objects or their fragments.

Titan is Saturn's largest moon and the only moon in the solar system known to have clouds, a dense atmosphere, and liquid lakes. The diameter of its solid body is 5,150 km (3,200 miles), which makes it, after Jupiter's

Ganymede, the second largest moon in the solar system. Its relatively low mean density of 1.88 grams per cubic cm implies that its interior is a mixture of rocky materials (silicates) and ices, the latter likely being mostly water ice mixed with frozen ammonia and methane.

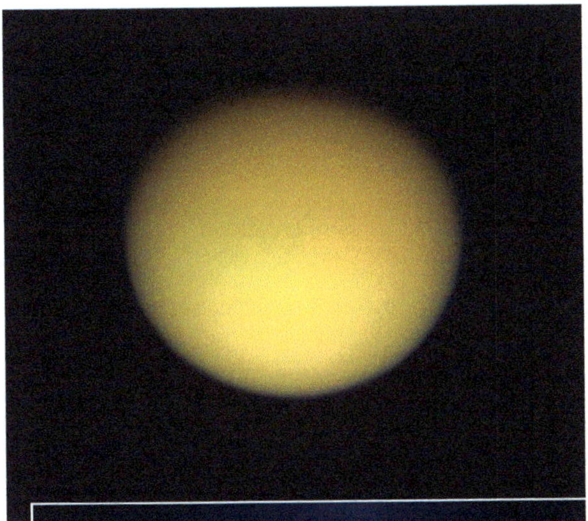

Global view of Titan, from the Cassini orbiter, February 15, 2005.

Titan's atmosphere, which has a surface pressure of 1.5 bars (50 percent greater than on Earth's surface), is predominantly nitrogen with about 5 percent methane and traces of a variety of other carbon-containing compounds.

Its surface, veiled in a thick brownish red haze, remained largely a mystery until exploration of the Saturnian system by Cassini-Huygens. The spacecraft's observations showed Titan to have a complex surface topography sculpted by precipitation, flowing liquids, wind, a few impacts, and possible volcanic and tectonic activity—many of the same processes that have shaped Earth's surface.

Saturn's other moons are much smaller than Titan and, except for Enceladus, possess no detectable atmospheres. (Cassini detected a localized water-vapour atmosphere in the vicinity of Enceladus's south polar hot spot.) Their low mean densities (between 1 and 1.5 grams per cubic cm), as well as spectroscopic analyses of their surface solids, indicate that they are rich in ices, probably mostly water ice perhaps mixed with ices of more-volatile substances such as carbon dioxide and ammonia. At Saturn's distance from the Sun, the ices are so cold that they behave mechanically like rock and can retain impact craters. As a result, the surfaces of these moons bear a superficial resemblance to the cratered rocky surface of Earth's Moon, but there are important differences.

Image of Mimas, backdropped by Saturn's hazy atmosphere.

Mimas reveals a heavily cratered surface similar in appearance to the lunar highlands, but it also possesses one of the largest impact structures, in relation to the body's size, in the solar system. The crater Herschel, named in honour of Mimas's discoverer, the 19th-century English astronomer William Herschel, is 130 km (80 miles) across, one-third the diameter of Mimas itself. It is roughly 10 km (6 miles) deep and has outer walls about 5 km (3 miles) high.

The surface of Enceladus reflects more light than newly fallen snow. Voyager images showed many regions with few large craters. The presence of smooth, crater-free areas and extensive ridged plains gave convincing evidence that fairly recent internal activity, possibly within the last 100 million years, has caused widespread melting and resurfacing. Spectral data from Cassini show that Enceladus's surface is almost pure water ice. The moon's south polar hot spot is at a temperature of 140 K (−208 °F, −133 °C), far hotter than is predicted from solar heating alone; the region also exhibits enigmatic geologic structures dubbed "tiger stripes." The water ice particles that form the E ring are being expelled

View of Enceladus, showing crater-free portions of the surface, possibly indicative of resurfacing by liquid water from the interior.

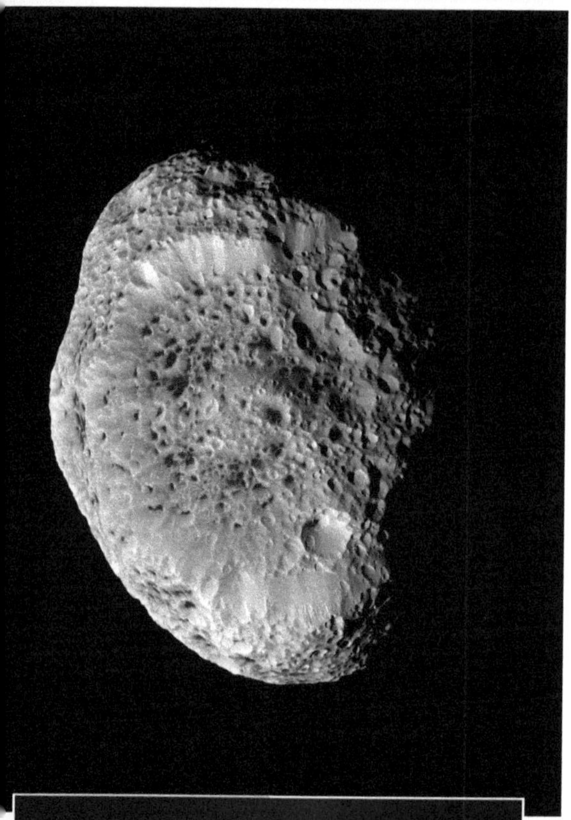

Saturn's impact-scarred moon Hyperion. Hyperion's interior may be a loose agglomeration of ice blocks interspersed with voids.

from Enceladus in plumes from the tiger stripes at the rate of about 1,000 metric tons per year. The particles have sizes in the range of one micrometre and could persist for only a few thousand years. Thus, the events on Enceladus that have produced the present ring must have been occurring within the recent past. About 30–40 km (19–25 miles) beneath the plumes is likely a subsurface ocean covering the entire moon with hydrothermal vents on its bottom.

Tethys, although larger than Enceladus, shows little evidence of internal activity. Its heavily cratered surface appears quite old, although it displays subtle features indicative of creep or viscous flow in its icy crust. Dione and Rhea have heavily cratered surfaces similar to the lunar highlands, but with bright patches that may be freshly exposed ice. Although Dione is smaller than Rhea, it has more evidence of recent internal activity, including resurfaced plains and fracture systems.

The surface of Iapetus shows a striking difference in reflectivity between its leading and trailing hemispheres. The leading hemisphere is remarkably dark, the darkest material concentrated at the apex of orbital motion. Cassini spectral data show the presence of carbon dioxide, organics, and cyanide compounds. The trailing hemisphere, which is as much as 10 times more reflective than the leading one, is heavily cratered and is mostly water ice. The reflectivity difference is caused by dark material from the Phoebe dust ring collecting on the leading hemisphere of Iapetus and absorbing more sunlight, which heats up this region. Any water ice there turns to water vapour, which condenses onto the trailing hemisphere and freezes. The low mean density of Iapetus suggests that the moon as a whole is mostly water ice.

CHAPTER 3

URANUS: AN ICE GIANT

Uranus, named for the personification of heaven and the son and husband of Gaea in Greek mythology, is just barely visible to the unaided eye at its brightest. The planet was not known to ancient astronomers. It was seen in early telescopes several times but was thought to be just another star. In 1781, as part of a telescopic survey of the stars, English astronomer William Herschel discovered "a curious either nebulous star or perhaps a comet." This unusual object soon proved to be a planet, the first to be identified in modern times.

Uranus is the seventh planet from the Sun, with more than two dozen moons and a system of narrow rings. Although it is not as big as Jupiter or Saturn, more than 60 Earths would fit inside it. The planet is most similar in size and composition to Neptune, its outer neighbour. Like Neptune, Uranus is blue-green because of the small amount of methane in its atmosphere.

Its mean distance from the Sun is nearly 2.9 billion km (1.8 billion miles), more than 19 times as far as is

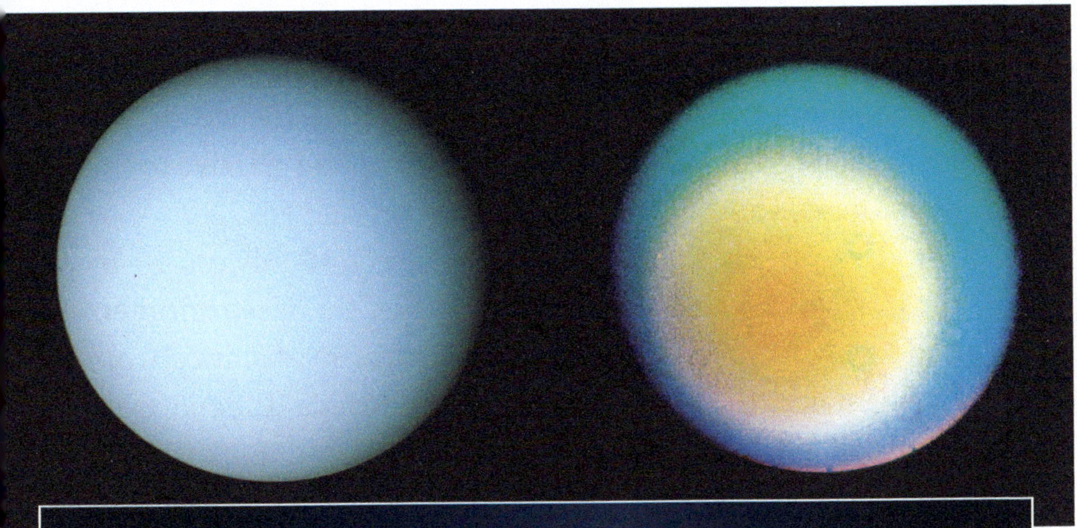

Two views of the southern hemisphere of Uranus. In a colour-enhanced view *(right)*, small ring-shaped features are artifacts arising from dust in the spacecraft's camera.

Earth, and it never approaches Earth more closely than about 2.7 billion km (1.7 billion miles). Its relatively low density (only about 1.3 times that of water) and large size (four times the radius of Earth) indicate that, like the other giant planets, Uranus is composed primarily of hydrogen, helium, water, and other volatile compounds; also like its kin, Uranus has no solid surface. Methane in the Uranian atmosphere absorbs the red wavelengths of sunlight, giving the planet its blue-green colour.

Most of the planets rotate on an axis that is more or less perpendicular to the plane of their respective orbits around the Sun. But Uranus's axis lies almost parallel to its orbital plane, which means that the planet spins nearly on its side, its poles taking turns pointing toward the Sun as the planet travels in its orbit. In addition, the axis of the planet's magnetic field is substantially tipped relative to the rotation axis and offset from the planet's centre.

Uranus has been visited by a spacecraft only once—by the U.S. Voyager 2 probe in 1986. Before then, astronomers had known little about the planet, since its distance from Earth makes the study of its visible surface difficult even with the most powerful telescopes available. Earth-based attempts to measure a property as basic as the planetary rotation period had produced widely differing values, ranging from 24 to 13 hours, until Voyager 2 finally established a 17.24-hour rotation period for the Uranian interior. Since Voyager's encounter, advances in Earth-based observational technology have added to knowledge of the Uranian system.

ASTRONOMICAL DATA OF URANUS

At Uranus's distance from the Sun, the planet takes slightly more than 84 Earth years, essentially an entire human life span, to complete one orbit. The eccentricity of its orbit is low—that is, its orbit deviates little from a perfect circle—and the inclination of the orbit to the ecliptic—the plane of Earth's orbit and nearly the plane of the solar system in general—is less than 1°. Low orbital eccentricity and inclination are characteristic of the planets of the solar system, with the notable exceptions of Mercury and Pluto. Scientists believe that collisions and gaseous drag removed energy from the orbits while the planets were forming and so reduced the eccentricities and inclinations to their present values. Thus, Uranus formed with the other planets soon after the birth of the Sun nearly 4.6 billion years ago.

Uranus and its neighbour Neptune, the next planet outward from the Sun, are nearly twins in size. Measured at the level of the atmosphere at which the pressure is one bar (equivalent to Earth's sea-level pressure), Uranus's equatorial radius of 25,559 km (15,882 miles) is 3.2 percent greater than that of Neptune. But Uranus has only 85 percent the mass of Neptune and thus is significantly less dense. The difference in their bulk densities—1.285 and 1.64 grams per cubic cm, respectively—reveals a fundamental difference in composition and internal structure. Although Uranus and Neptune are significantly larger than the terrestrial planets, their radii are less than half those of the largest planets, Jupiter and Saturn.

Because Uranus's spin axis is not perfectly parallel to the ecliptic, one of its poles is directed above the ecliptic and the other below it. (The terms above and below refer to the same sides of the ecliptic as Earth's North and South poles, respectively.) According to international convention, the north pole of a planet is defined as the pole that is above the ecliptic regardless of the direction in which the planet is spinning. In terms of this definition, Uranus spins clockwise, or in a retrograde fashion, about its north pole, which is opposite to the prograde spin of Earth and most of the other planets. When Voyager 2 flew by Uranus in 1986, the north pole was in darkness, and the Sun was almost directly overhead at the south pole. In 42 years, or one-half the Uranian year, the Sun will have moved to a position nearly overhead at the north pole.

The prevailing theory is that the severe tilt arose during the final stages of planetary accretion when bodies comparable in size to the present planets collided in a series of violent events that knocked Uranus on its side. An alternate theory is that a Mars-sized moon, orbiting Uranus in a direction opposite to the planet's spin, eventually crashed into the planet and knocked it on its side.

Uranus's rotation period of 17.24 hours was inferred when Voyager 2 detected radio wave emissions with that period coming from charged particles trapped in the planet's magnetic field. Subsequent direct measurements of the field showed that it is tilted at an angle of 58.6° relative to the rotation axis and that it turns with the same 17.24-hour period. Because the field is thought to be generated in the electrically conducting interior of the planet, the 17.24-hour period is assumed to be that of the interior. The relatively fast rotation causes an oblateness, or flattening of the planet's poles, such that the polar radius is about 2.3

percent smaller than the equatorial radius. Winds in the atmosphere cause cloud markings on the visible surface to rotate around the planet with periods ranging from 18 hours near the equator to slightly more than 14 hours at higher latitudes.

THE ATMOSPHERE OF URANUS

Molecular hydrogen and atomic helium are the two main constituents of the Uranian atmosphere. Methane absorbs strongly at near-infrared wavelengths, and it dominates that part of the spectrum of reflected light even though the number of methane molecules is only 2.3 percent of the total.

On average, Uranus radiates the same amount of energy as an ideal, perfectly absorbing surface at a temperature of 59.1 kelvins (K; −353 °F, −214 °C). This radiation temperature is equal to the physical temperature of the atmosphere at a pressure of about 0.4 bar. Temperature decreases with decreasing pressure—i.e., with increasing altitude—throughout this portion of the atmosphere to the 70-millibar level, where it is about 52 K (−366 °F, −221 °C), the coldest temperature in Uranus's atmosphere. From this point upward the temperature rises again until it reaches 750 K (890 °F, 480 °C) in the exosphere—the top of the atmosphere at a distance of 1.1 Uranian radii from the planetary centre—where pressures are on the order of a trillionth of a bar. The cause of the high exospheric temperatures remains to be determined, but it may involve a combination of ultraviolet absorption, electron bombardment, and inability of the gas to radiate at infrared wavelengths.

Although Uranus appears nearly featureless to the eye, extreme-contrast-enhanced images from Voyager 2 and more-recent observations from Earth reveal faint cloud bands oriented parallel to the equator. The same kind of zonal flow dominates the atmospheric circulation of Jupiter and Saturn, whose rotational axes are much less tilted than Uranus's axis and thus whose seasonal changes in solar illumination are much different. Apparently, rotation of the planet itself and not the distribution of absorbed sunlight controls the cloud patterns. Rotation manifests itself through the Coriolis force, an effect that causes material moving on a rotating planet to appear to be deflected to either the right or the left depending on the hemisphere—northern or southern—being considered. In terms of cloud patterns, therefore, Uranus looks like a tipped-over version of Jupiter or Saturn.

The wind is the motion of the atmosphere relative to the rotating planet. At high latitudes on Uranus, this relative motion is in the direction of the planet's rotation. At equatorial latitudes the relative motion is in the opposite direction. Uranus is like Earth in this regard. On Earth these directions are called east and west, respectively, but the more-general terms are prograde and retrograde.

The winds that exist on Uranus are several times stronger than on Earth. The wind is 200 metres per second (720 km [450 miles] per hour) prograde at a latitude of 55° S and 110 metres per second (400 km [250 miles] per hour) retrograde at the equator. Neptune's equatorial winds are also retrograde, but those of Jupiter and Saturn are prograde. No satisfactory theory exists to explain these differences.

Uranus has no large spots like Jupiter's long-lived Great Red Spot or the Great Dark Spot observed on Neptune by Voyager 2 in 1989. Voyager's measurements of the wind profile on Uranus came from just four small spots whose visual contrast was no more than 2 or 3 percent relative to the surrounding atmosphere. Because the giant planets have no solid surfaces, the spots must represent atmospheric storms. For reasons that are not clear, Uranus seems to have the smallest number of storms of any of the giant planets.

THE MAGNETIC FIELD AND MAGNETOSPHERE

Like the other giant planets, Uranus has a magnetic field that is generated by convection currents in an electrically conducting interior. The dipole field, which resembles the field of a small but intense bar magnet, has a strength of 0.23 gauss in its equatorial plane at a distance of one Uranian equatorial radius from the centre. The polarity of the field is oriented in the same direction as Earth's present field—i.e., an ordinary magnetic compass would point toward the counterclockwise rotation pole, which for Earth is the North Pole.

The magnetic field is unusual not only because of its tilt and offset but also because of the relatively large size of its small-scale components. This "roughness" suggests that the field is generated at shallow depths within the planet, because small-scale components of a field die out rapidly above the electrically conducting region. Thus, the interior of Uranus must become electrically conducting closer to the surface than on Jupiter, Saturn, and Earth. This inference is consistent with what is known about Uranus's internal composition, which must be mostly water, methane, and ammonia in order to match the average density of the planet. Water and ammonia dissociate into positive and negative ions—which are electrically conducting—at relatively low pressures and temperatures. As on Jupiter, Saturn, and Earth, the field is generated by fluid motions in the conducting layers, but on Uranus the layers are not as deep.

As is the case for the other planets that have magnetic fields, Uranus's field repels the solar wind, the stream of charged particles flowing outward from the Sun. The planetary magnetosphere—a huge region of space containing charged particles that are bound to the magnetic field—surrounds the planet and extends downwind from it. On the upwind side, facing the Sun, the magnetopause—the boundary between the magnetosphere and the solar wind—is 18 Uranian radii (460,000 km [286,000 miles]) from the centre of the planet.

The particles trapped within the Uranian magnetosphere comprise protons and electrons, which indicate that the planet's upper atmosphere is supplying most of the material. There is no evidence of helium, which might originate with the solar wind, or of heavier ions, which might come from the Uranian moons. Because the largest Uranian moons orbit within the magnetosphere, they absorb some of the trapped particles. The particles behave as if they were attached to the magnetic field lines, so that those lines intersecting a moon in its orbit have fewer trapped particles than neighbouring field lines.

As is the case for Jupiter and Saturn, charged particles from the Uranian magnetosphere impinge on the upper atmosphere and produce auroras. Auroral heating can just barely account for the high temperature of Uranus's exosphere. One effect of the high temperature is that the atmosphere expands outward into the region occupied by ring particles and, by increasing drag, severely limits their orbital lifetime. This puts constraints on the age of the present material in the rings.

THE INTERIOR

Although Uranus has a somewhat lower density than Jupiter, it has a higher proportion of elements heavier than hydrogen and helium. Jupiter's greater mass (by a factor of 22) leads to a greater gravitational force and thus greater self-compression than for Uranus. This additional compression adds to Jupiter's bulk density. If Uranus were made of the same proportions of material as Jupiter, it would be considerably less dense than it is.

Different models proposed for the Uranian interior assume different ratios of rock (silicates and metals), ices (water, methane, and ammonia), and gases (essentially hydrogen and helium). At the high temperatures and pressures within the giant planets, the "ices" will in fact be liquids. To be consistent with the bulk density data, the mass of rock plus ice must constitute roughly 80 percent of the total mass of Uranus, compared with 10 percent for Jupiter and 2 percent for a mixture of the Sun's composition. In all models Uranus is a fluid planet, with the gaseous higher atmosphere gradually merging with the liquid interior. Pressure at the centre of the planet is about five megabars.

Scientists have obtained more information about the interior by comparing a given model's response to centrifugal forces, which arise from the planet's rotation, with the response of the actual planet measured by Voyager 2. This response is expressed in terms of the planet's oblateness. By measuring the degree of flattening at the poles and relating it to the speed of rotation, scientists can infer the density distribution inside the planet. For two planets with the same mass and bulk density, the planet with more of its mass concentrated close to the centre would be less flattened by rotation. Before the Voyager mission, it was difficult to choose between models in which the three components—rock, ice, and gas—were separated into distinct layers and those in which the ice and gas were well mixed. From the combination of large oblateness and comparatively slow rotation for Uranus measured by Voyager, it appears that the ice and gas are well mixed and a rocky core is small or nonexistent.

Unlike the other three giant planets, Uranus does not radiate a substantial amount of excess internal heat. The total heat output is determined from the planet's measured infrared emissions, while the heat input is determined from the fraction of incident sunlight that is absorbed—i.e., not scattered back into space. For Uranus the ratio of the two is between 1.00 and 1.14, which means that its internal energy source supplies, at most, 14 percent more energy than the planet receives from the Sun. (The equivalent ratios for the other giant planets are greater than 1.7.) The small terrestrial planets—Mercury, Venus, Earth, and Mars—generate relatively little internal heat; the heat flow from Earth's interior, for example, is only about a ten-thousandth of what it receives from the Sun.

It is not clear why Uranus has such a low internal heat output compared with the other Jovian planets. All the planets should have started warm, since gravitational energy was transformed into heat during planetary accretion. Over the age of the solar system, Earth and the other smaller objects have lost most of their heat of formation. Being massive objects with cold surfaces, however, the giant planets store heat well and radiate poorly. Therefore, they should have retained large fractions of their heat of formation, which should still be escaping today. Chance events (such as collisions with large bodies) experienced by some planets but not others at the time of their formation and the resulting differences in internal structure are one explanation proposed to explain differences among the giant planets such as the anomalous heat output of Uranus.

Uranus's 27 known moons are accompanied by at least 10 narrow rings. Each of the countless particles that make up the rings can be considered a tiny moon in its own orbit. In general, the rings are located closest to the planet, some small moons orbit just outside the rings, the largest moons orbit beyond them, and other small moons orbit much farther out. The orbits of the outermost group of moons are eccentric (elongated) and highly inclined to Uranus's equatorial plane. The other moons and the rings are essentially coplanar with the equator.

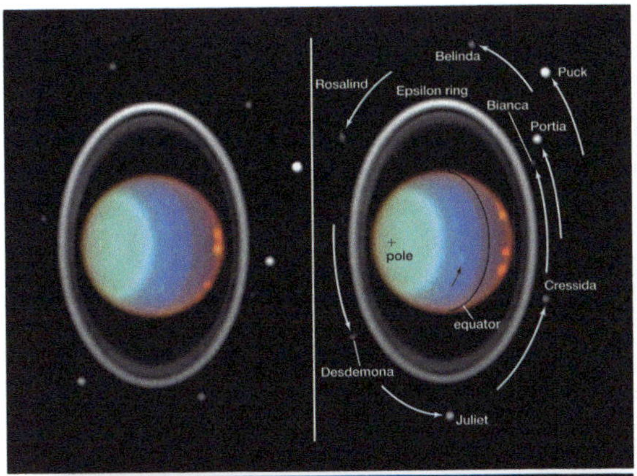

Uranus's southern hemisphere. Comparison of the images reveals the orbital motion of the moons along Uranus's equatorial plane and the counterclockwise rotation of clouds.

MOONS OF URANUS

Uranus's five largest moons range from about 240 to 800 km (150 to 500 miles) in radius. All were discovered telescopically from Earth, four of them before the 20th century. Ten small inner moons were found by Voyager 2 in 1985–86. They are estimated to be between about 10 and 80 km (6 and 50 miles) in radius, and they orbit the planet at distances between 49,800 and 86,000 km (31,000 and 53,500 miles). The innermost moon, Cordelia, orbits just inside the outermost rings, Lambda and Epsilon. An 11th tiny inner moon, Perdita, photographed by Voyager near the orbit of Belinda, remained unnoticed in the images until 1999 and was not confirmed until 2003. Two additional inner moons—Cupid, near Belinda's orbit, and the other, Mab, near Puck's—were discovered in observations from Earth in 2003. All 18 of the above are regular, having prograde, low-inclination, and low-eccentricity orbits with respect to the planet.

Nine small outer moons in roughly the same size range as the Voyager finds were discovered from Earth beginning in 1997. These are irregular satellites, having highly elliptical orbits that are inclined at large angles to the planet's equator; all but one also orbit in the retrograde direction. Their mean distances from the planet lie between 4 million and 21 million km (2.5 million and 13 million miles), which is 7–36 times the distance of the outermost known regular moon, Oberon. The irregular moons likely were captured into orbits around Uranus after the planet formed. The regular moons probably formed in their equatorial orbits at the same time that the planet formed.

The four largest moons—Titania, Oberon, Umbriel, and Ariel, in order of decreasing size—have densities of 1.4–1.7 grams per cubic cm. This range is only slightly greater than the density of a hypothetical object that would be obtained by cooling a mixture of solar composition and removing all the gaseous components. The object that remained would be 60 percent ice and 40 percent rock. In contrast to these four is Miranda, the fifth largest Uranian moon, but only half the size of Ariel or Umbriel. Like the smaller moons of Saturn, Miranda has a density (1.2 grams per cubic cm) that is slightly below the solar composition value, which indicates a higher ice-to-rock ratio.

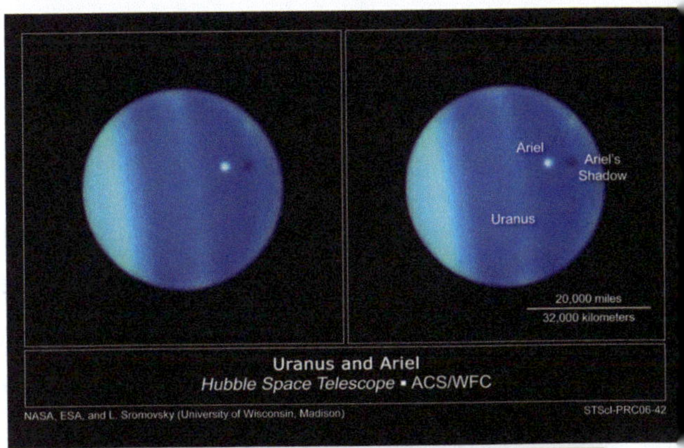

Ariel (white dot) and its shadow (black dot) crossing the face of Uranus in an image captured by the Hubble Space Telescope.

Water ice shows up in the surface spectra of the five major moons. Because the reflectivities of the moons are lower than that of pure ice, the obvious implication is that their surfaces consist of dirty water ice. The composition of the dark component is unknown, but, at wavelengths other than those of water, the surface spectra seem evenly dark, indicating a neutral gray colour and thus ruling out material such as iron-bearing minerals, which would impart a reddish tinge. One possibility is carbon, originating from inside the moons in question or from Uranus's rings, which could have released methane gas that later decomposed to produce solid carbon when bombarded by charged particles and solar ultraviolet light.

Titania, the largest moon of Uranus.

The surfaces of the major moons are porous and highly insulating. Virtually all of what is known about the distinctive surface characters of Uranus's major moons comes from Voyager 2, which sped past them in a few hours and imaged only their sunlit southern hemispheres. Oberon and particularly Umbriel display dense populations of large impact craters, similar to the highlands of Earth's Moon and many of the oldest terrains in the solar system. In contrast, Titania and Ariel have far fewer large craters (in the range of 50–100 km [30–60 miles] in diameter) but have comparable numbers in the smaller size ranges. The large craters are thought to date back to the early history of the solar system more than four billion years ago, when large planetesimals still existed, whereas the smaller ones are thought to reflect more-recent events including, perhaps, the impacts of objects knocked loose from other moons in the Uranian system. Thus, the surfaces of Titania and Ariel must be younger than those of Oberon and Umbriel. These differences, which do not follow an obvious pattern with respect to either the moons' distances from Uranus or their sizes, are largely unexplained.

Volcanic deposits observed on the major moons are

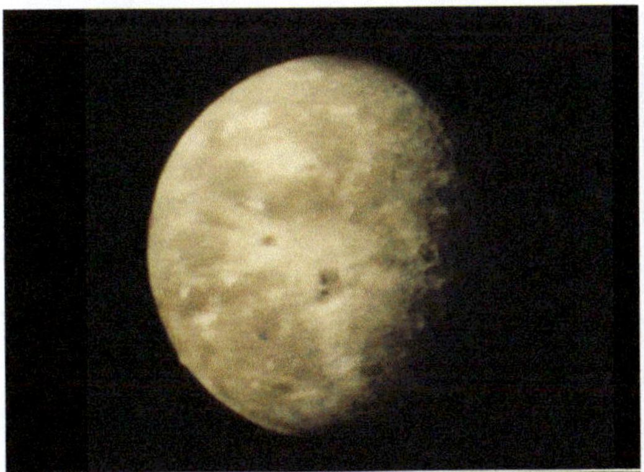

Oberon, outermost of the five major moons of Uranus. The image shows several large impact craters surrounded by bright rays of ejecta.

generally flat, with lobed edges and surface ripples characteristic of fluid flow. Some of the deposits are bright, while some are dark. Because of the very low temperatures expected for the outer solar system, the erupting fluid was probably a water-ammonia mixture with a melting point well below that of pure water ice. Brightness differences could indicate differences in the composition of the erupting fluid or in the history of the surface.

Riftlike canyons seen on the major moons imply extension and fracturing of their surfaces. Miranda's canyons are the most spectacular, some being as much as 80 km (50 miles) wide and 15 km (9 miles) deep. The rupturing of the crust was caused by an expansion in the volume of the moons, inferred to be in the range of 1–2 percent, except for Miranda, for which the expansion is thought to be 6 percent. Miranda's expansion could be explained if all the water making up its interior were once liquid and then froze after the crust had formed. Freezing under low pressure, the water would have expanded and thereby stretched and shattered the

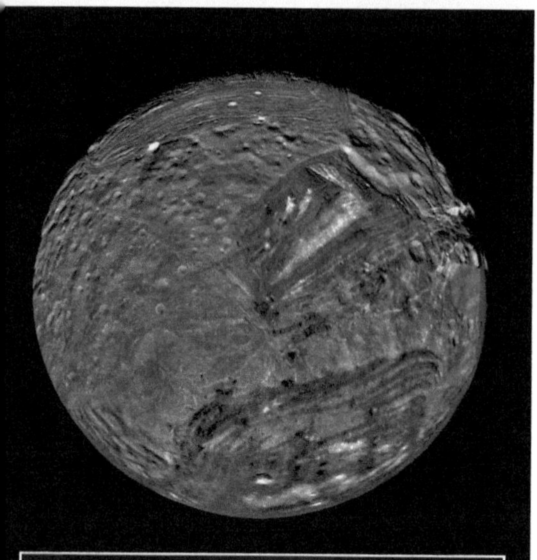

Miranda. In this south polar view, old, heavily cratered terrain is interspersed with large sharp-edged patches of young, lightly cratered regions.

surface. The presence of liquid water on the surface at any stage of the moon's history seems unlikely.

Miranda has the jumbled appearance of an object formed from separate pieces that did not totally merge. The basic surface is heavily cratered, but it is interrupted by three lightly cratered regions that astronomers have named coronae (but which are not related geologically to surface features of Venus of the same name). These are fairly squarish, roughly the length of one Miranda radius on a side, and are surrounded by parallel bands that curve around the edges. The boundaries where the coronae meet the cratered terrain are sharp. The coronae are unlike any features found elsewhere in the solar system. Whether they reflect a heterogeneous origin for the moon, a giant impact that shattered it, or a unique pattern of eruptions from its interior is not known.

THE RING SYSTEM

The rings of Uranus are narrow and fairly opaque. Observed widths are simply the radial distances between the beginning and the end of the individual dimming events. Equivalent widths are the product (more precisely, the integral) of the radial distance and the fraction of starlight blocked. The fact that the equivalent widths are generally less than the observed widths indicates that the rings are not completely opaque.

Combining the brightness of the rings observed in Voyager images with the equivalent widths from occultations shows that the ring particles reflect less than 5 percent of the incident sunlight. Their nearly flat reflectance spectrum means that the particles are basically gray in colour. Ordinary soot, which is mostly carbon, is the closest terrestrial analogue. It is not known whether the carbon comes from darkening of methane by particle bombardment or is intrinsic to the ring particles.

The scattering effects on Voyager's radio signal propagated through the rings to Earth revealed that the rings consist of mostly large particles, objects greater than 140 cm (4.6 feet) across. Scattering of sunlight when Voyager was on the far side of the rings and aiming its camera back toward the Sun also revealed small dust particles in the micrometre size range. Only a small amount of dust was found in the

DISCOVERY OF THE RINGS

The rings of Uranus were the first to be found around a planet other than Saturn. The American astronomer James L. Elliot and colleagues discovered the ring system from Earth in 1977, nine years before the Voyager 2 encounter, during a stellar occultation by Uranus—i.e., when the planet passed between a star and Earth, temporarily blocking the star's light. Unexpectedly, they observed the star to dim briefly five times at some considerable distance above Uranus's atmosphere both before and after the planet occulted the star.

The dips in brightness indicated that the planet was encircled by five narrow rings. Later Earth-based observations revealed four additional rings. Voyager 2 detected a 10th ring and found indications of others. Outward from Uranus, the 10 are named 6, 5, 4, Alpha, Beta, Eta, Gamma, Delta, Lambda, and Epsilon. The cumbersome nomenclature arose as the new rings were found in places that did not fit the original nomenclature.

main rings. Most of the microscopic particles were instead distributed in the spaces between the main rings, which suggests that the rings are losing mass as a result of collisions.

The lifetime of the dust in orbit around Uranus is limited by drag exerted by the planet's extended atmosphere and by the radiation pressure of sunlight; the dust particles are driven to lower orbits and eventually fall into the Uranian atmosphere. The calculated orbital lifetimes are so short—1,000 years—that the dust must be rapidly and continually created. Uranus's atmospheric drag appears to be so large that the present rings themselves may be short-lived. If so, the rings did not form with Uranus, and their origin and history are unknown.

Collisions between the tightly packed ring particles would naturally lead to an increase in the radial width of the rings. Moons more massive than the rings can halt this spreading in a process called shepherding. Certain orbits that lie inside or outside the orbit of a given ring are at the proper radius for a moon in such an orbit to establish a stable dynamic resonance with the ring particles. The condition for the resonance is that the orbital periods of the moon and the ring particles are related to each other in the ratio of small whole numbers. In this kind of relationship, as the moon and the particles pass one another periodically, they interact gravitationally in a way that tends to maintain the regularity of the encounters.

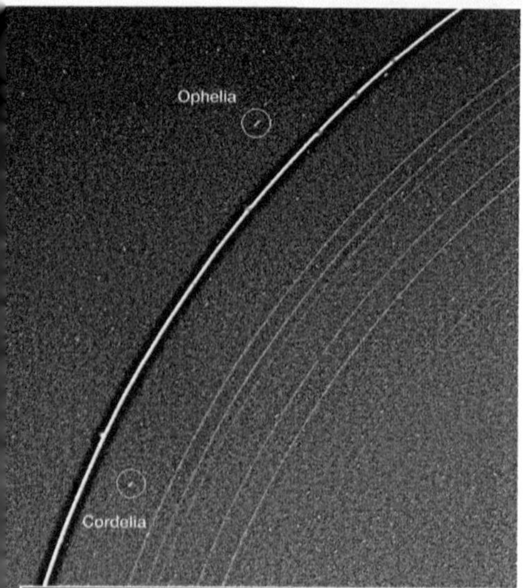

Portion of Uranus's ring system with the bright Epsilon ring flanked by its two shepherd moons, Cordelia and Ophelia.

The moon exerts a net torque on the ring, and, as the moon and ring exchange angular momentum, energy is dissipated by collisions among the ring particles. The outcome is that the moon and ring particles repel each other. Whichever body is in the outer orbit moves outward, while the one in the inner orbit moves inward. Because the moon is much more massive than the ring, it prevents the ring from spreading across the radius at which resonance occurs. A pair of shepherd moons, one on either side of a ring, can maintain its narrow width.

Voyager 2 found that the innermost two moons, Cordelia and Ophelia, orbit on either side of the Epsilon ring at exactly the right radii required for shepherding. Shepherds for the other rings were not observed, perhaps because the moons are too small to be seen in the Voyager images. Small moons may also be reservoirs that supply the dust leaving the ring system.

CHAPTER 4

Big, Blue Neptune

In the mid-1800s several astronomers began looking for a planet beyond Uranus, in part because Uranus did not move along its orbit exactly as expected. Scientists thought that these slight differences could be caused by the gravitational pull of another planet, and they were right. Neptune's discovery was a remarkable combination of the application of solid Newtonian physics and a belief in a numerological scheme that later proved to be scientifically unfounded. Several people can be credited with the discovery. John Couch Adams and Urbain-Jean-Joseph Le Verrier independently calculated the planet's probable location, while in 1846 Johann Gottfried Galle and his assistant Heinrich Louis d'Arrest were the first to identify it in the night sky.

Neptune is named for the Roman god of the sea, who is identified with the Greek deity Poseidon, a son of the Titan Cronus (the Roman god Saturn) and a brother of Zeus (the Roman god Jupiter). It is the eighth and farthest

Clouds in Neptune's atmosphere. The Great Dark Spot is centre left. Accompanying it are bright, wispy clouds thought to comprise methane ice crystals.

planet from the Sun. It is always more than 4 billion km (2.5 billion miles) from Earth, making it too far to be seen with the unaided eye. It was the second planet, after Uranus, to be discovered through a telescope but the first planet to be found by people specifically searching for one.

Relatively little was known about Neptune until the Voyager 2 spacecraft—the only mission to the planet—flew by it in 1989. The world that Voyager uncovered is stormy and windswept, with a vivid blue hue. Its highly active atmosphere is surprising, since it receives so little sunlight to power its weather systems. Like the other giant outer planets, Neptune has no solid surface. It also has a system of rings and more than a dozen moons.

Neptune is almost four times the size of Earth but slightly smaller than Uranus, which makes it the smallest in diameter of the four outer planets. It is more massive than Uranus, however, having a density roughly 25 percent higher. Like the other giant planets, Neptune consists primarily of hydrogen, helium, water, and other volatile compounds, along with rocky material, and it has no solid surface. It receives less than half as much sunlight as Uranus, but heat escaping from its interior makes Neptune slightly warmer than Uranus. The heat liberated may also be responsible for the storminess in Neptune's atmosphere, which exhibits the fastest winds seen on any planet in the solar system.

Neptune has 14 moons (natural satellites), only two of which had been discovered before the Voyager 2 spacecraft flew past the planet in 1989, and a system of rings, which had been unconfirmed until Voyager's visit. As is the case for Uranus, most of what astronomers know about Neptune, including its rotation period and the existence and characteristics of its magnetic field and magnetosphere, was learned from a single spacecraft encounter. In recent years new knowledge of the Neptunian system has come as a result of advances in Earth-based observational technology.

NEPTUNE: AN OVERVIEW

Having an orbital period of 164.79 years, Neptune has circled the Sun only once since its discovery in September 1846. Consequently, astronomers expect to be making refinements in calculating its orbital size and shape well into the 21st century. Voyager 2's encounter with Neptune resulted in a small upward revision of the planet's estimated mean distance from the Sun, which is now thought to be 4,498,250,000 km (2,795,083,000 miles). Its orbital eccentricity of 0.0086 is the second lowest of the planets; only Venus's orbit is more circular. Neptune's rotation axis is tipped toward its orbital plane by 29.6°, somewhat larger than Earth's 23.4°. As on Earth, the axial tilt gives rise to seasons on Neptune, and, because of the circularity of Neptune's orbit, the seasons (and the seasons of its moons) are of nearly equal length, each nearly 41 years in duration.

Neptune's rotation period was established when Voyager 2 detected radio bursts associated with the planet's magnetic field and having a period of 16.11 hours. This value was inferred to be the rotation period at the level of the planet's interior where the magnetic field is rooted. Neptune's equatorial diameter measured at the one-bar pressure level is 49,528 km (30,775 miles), which is only about 3 percent shy of the diameter of Uranus. Because of a flattening of the poles caused by the planet's relatively fast rotation, Neptune's polar diameter is 848 km (527 miles) less than its diameter at the equator. Although Neptune occupies a little less volume than Uranus, owing to its greater density—1.64 grams per cubic cm, compared with about 1.3 for Uranus—Neptune's mass is 18 percent higher.

NEPTUNE'S ATMOSPHERE

Like the other giant planets, Neptune's outer atmosphere is composed predominantly of hydrogen and helium. Near the one-bar pressure level in the atmosphere, these two gases contribute nearly 98 percent of the atmospheric molecules. Most of the remaining molecules consist of methane gas. Hydrogen and helium are nearly invisible, but methane strongly absorbs red light. Sunlight reflected off Neptune's clouds therefore exits the atmosphere with most of its red colours removed and so has a bluish cast. Although Uranus's blue-green colour is also the result of atmospheric methane, Neptune's colour is a more vivid, brighter blue, presumably an effect of the presence of an unidentified atmospheric gas.

The temperature of Neptune's atmosphere varies with altitude. A minimum temperature of about 50 kelvins (K; −370 °F, −223 °C) occurs at a pressure near 0.1 bar. The temperature increases with decreasing pressure—i.e., with increasing altitude—to about 750 K (890 °F, 480 °C) at a pressure of a hundred-billionth of a bar, which corresponds to an altitude of 2,000 km (1,240 miles) as measured from the one-bar level, and it remains uniform above that altitude.

Neptune is more than 50 percent farther from the Sun than is Uranus and so receives less than half the sunlight of the latter. Yet the effective temperatures of these two giant planets are nearly equal. Uranus and Neptune each reflect—and hence also must absorb—about the same proportion of the sunlight that reaches them. As a result of processes not fully understood, Neptune emits more than twice the energy that it receives from the Sun. The added energy is generated in Neptune's interior. Uranus, by contrast, has little energy escaping from its interior.

At the one-bar reference level, the mean temperature of Neptune's atmosphere is roughly 74 K (−326 °F, −199 °C). Atmospheric temperatures are a few degrees warmer at the equator and poles than at mid-latitudes. This is probably an indication that air currents are rising near mid-latitudes and descending near the equator and poles. This vertical flow may extend to great heights within the atmosphere. A more vertically confined horizontal wind system exists near the cloud tops. As with the other giant planets, Neptune's atmospheric circulation exhibits zonal flow—the winds are constrained to blow generally along lines of constant latitude (east-west) and are relatively invariable with time.

Winds on Neptune range from about 100 metres per second (360 km [220 miles] per hour) in an easterly direction (prograde, or in the same direction as the planet's spin) near latitude 70° S to as high as 700 metres per second (2,520 km [1,570 miles] per hour) in a westerly direction (retrograde, or opposite to the planet's spin) near latitude 20° S.

The high winds and relatively large amount of escaping internal heat may be responsible for the turbulence observed in Neptune's visible atmosphere by Voyager 2. Two large dark ovals were clearly visible in Voyager images of Neptune's southern hemisphere. The largest, called the Great Dark Spot because of its similarity in latitude and shape to Jupiter's Great Red Spot, is comparable to Earth in size. It was near this storm system that the highest wind speeds were measured.

Jupiter's Great Red Spot has been seen in Earth-based telescopes for more than 150 years. Neptune's Great Dark Spot was expected by analogy to be similarly long-lived. Scientists thus were surprised by its absence from images of Neptune obtained by the Earth-orbiting Hubble Space Telescope in 1991, only two years after the Voyager flyby, just as they were by the appearance of a comparable dark spot in Neptune's northern hemisphere in 1994. Bright cloud features seen in the Voyager images are even more transient; they may be methane ice clouds created by strong upward motions of pockets of methane gas to higher, colder altitudes in the atmosphere, where the gas then condenses to ice crystals.

Neptune is the only giant planet to display cloud shadows cast by high dispersed clouds on a lower, more continuous cloud bank. The higher clouds, probably composed of methane ice crystals, are generally located 50–100 km

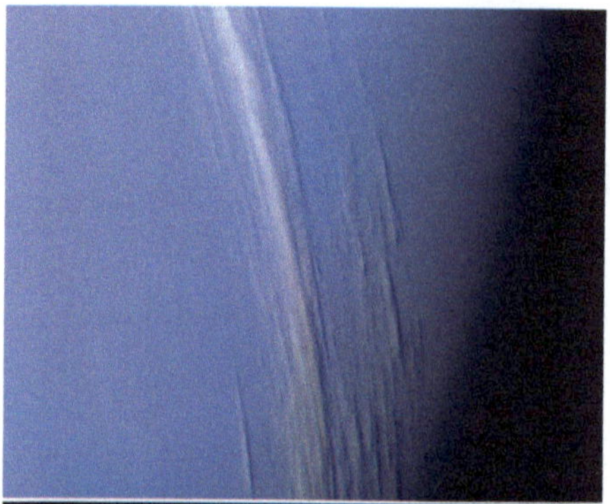

Clouds in Neptune's northern hemisphere. Illuminated by sunlight from the left, they cast shadows onto the underlying cloud deck.

(30–60 miles) above the main cloud deck, which may be composed of ice crystals of ammonia or hydrogen sulfide. Like the other giant planets, Neptune is thought to possess cloud layers at deeper levels, below those visible to Voyager's remote sensing instruments, but their composition is dependent on the relative amounts of gases composed of compounds of sulfur and nitrogen. Clouds of water ice are expected to occur at depths within Neptune's atmosphere where the pressure exceeds 100 bars.

THE MAGNETIC FIELD AND MAGNETOSPHERE OF NEPTUNE

Neptune, like most of the other planets in the solar system, possesses an internally generated magnetic field, first detected in 1989 by Voyager 2. Like Earth's magnetic field, Neptune's field can be represented approximately by that of a dipole (similar to a bar magnet), but its polarity is essentially opposite to that of Earth's present field. A magnetic compass on Neptune would point toward south instead of north.

Earth's field is thought to be generated by electric currents flowing in its liquid iron core, and electric currents flowing within the outer cores of liquid metallic hydrogen in Jupiter and Saturn may similarly be the source of their magnetic fields. The magnetic fields of Earth, Jupiter, and Saturn are relatively well centred within the respective planets and aligned within about 12° of the planetary rotation axes. Uranus and Neptune, by contrast, have magnetic fields that are tilted from their rotation axes by almost 59° and 47°, respectively. Furthermore, the fields are not internally well centred. Uranus's field is offset by 31 percent of the planet's radius. Neptune's field, having an offset of 55 percent of the radius, is centred in a portion of the interior that is actually closer to the cloud tops than to the planetary centre. The unusual configurations of the magnetic fields of Uranus and Neptune have led scientists to speculate that these fields may be generated in processes occurring in the upper layers of the planetary interiors.

The magnetic field of Neptune (and of the other planets) is approximately apple-shaped, with the stem end and the opposite end oriented in the directions of the magnetic poles. The solar wind, a stream of electrically charged particles that flows outward from the Sun, distorts that regular shape, compressing it on the sunward side of the planet and stretching it into a long tail in the direction away from the Sun.

Trapped within the magnetic field are charged particles, predominantly protons and electrons. The region of space dominated by Neptune's magnetic field and charged particles is called its magnetosphere. Because of the high tilt of Neptune's magnetic field, the particles trapped in the magnetosphere are repeatedly swept past the orbits of the moons and rings. Many of these particles may be absorbed by the moons and ring material, effectively emptying from the magnetosphere a large fraction of its charged particle content.

Neptune's magnetosphere is populated with fewer protons and electrons per unit volume than that of any other giant planet. Near the magnetic poles, the charged particles in the magnetosphere can travel along magnetic field lines into the atmosphere. As they collide with gases there, they cause those gases to fluoresce, resulting in classical, albeit weak, auroras.

The Origin of Neptune's Orbit

In the most commonly accepted model of the solar system's formation, the Nice Model (named after the French city where it was first postulated), the four giant planets—Jupiter, Saturn, Uranus, and Neptune—orbited between about 5 and 17 astronomical units (1 astronomical unit is about 150 million km [93 million miles], the mean distance of Earth from the Sun). The planets were in orbital resonances. For example, if Neptune was in the 3:4 resonance, for every three times Neptune orbited around the Sun, Uranus would orbit four. The planets orbited in a disk of planetesimals, small bodies left over from the formation of the solar system.

Gravitational interactions with these planetesimals, of which several hundred were the size of the dwarf planet Pluto, knocked the planets out of their orbital resonances and increased the eccentricity of their orbits. The orbits of the planets became unstable, and Saturn, Uranus, and Neptune migrated outward to their current positions. In some simulations, Uranus and Neptune even switch positions. (Jupiter migrated slightly inward.)

The planetesimal disk was dispersed, which caused the Late Heavy Bombardment, an event of heavy cratering on the inner terrestrial planets that happened about four billion years ago. A small remnant of the disk became the Kuiper belt, and some planetesimals were captured to became Neptune's Trojan asteroids.

NEPTUNE'S INTERIOR

Although Neptune has a mean density slightly less than 30 percent of Earth's, it is the densest of the giant planets. This implies that a larger percentage of Neptune's interior is composed of melted ices and molten rocky materials than is the case for the other giant planets.

The distribution of these heavier elements and compounds is poorly known. Voyager 2 data suggest that Neptune is unlikely to have a distinct inner core of molten rocky materials surrounded by an outer core of melted ices of methane, ammonia, and water. The relatively slow rotation of 16.11 hours measured by Voyager was about one hour longer than would be expected from such a layered interior model. Scientists have concluded that the heavier compounds and elements, rather than being centrally condensed, may be spread almost uniformly throughout the interior. In this respect, as in many others, Neptune resembles Uranus far more than it does the larger giants Jupiter and Saturn.

THE MOONS AND RINGS OF NEPTUNE

Neptune has at least 14 moons and six known narrow rings. Each of the myriad particles that constitute the rings can be considered a tiny moon in its own orbit. The four moons nearest the planet orbit within the ring system, where at least some of them may interact gravitationally with the ring particles, keeping them from spreading out.

Prior to Voyager 2's encounter, Neptune's only known moons were Triton, discovered visually through a telescope in 1846, and Nereid, discovered in telescopic photographs more than a century later, in 1949. (Neptune's moons are named after figures in Greek mythology usually connected with Poseidon [the Roman god Neptune] or with water.)

With a diameter nearly that of Earth's Moon, Triton is, by far, Neptune's largest satellite—more than six times the size of its largest known sibling, Proteus, discovered by Voyager 2 in 1989. Triton is the only large moon of the solar system that travels around its planet in retrograde fashion. Moreover, whereas the orbits of the largest moons in the solar system are inclined less than about 5° to their planet's equator, Triton's orbit is tilted more than 157° to Neptune's equator. Nereid, which revolves more than 15 times farther from Neptune on average than does Triton, has the most eccentric orbit of any known moon. At its greatest distance, Nereid is nearly seven times as far from Neptune as at its smallest distance. Even at its closest approach, Nereid is nearly four times the distance of Triton.

In 1989 Voyager's observations added six previously unknown moons to Neptune's system. All are less than half of Triton's distance from Neptune and are regular moons—

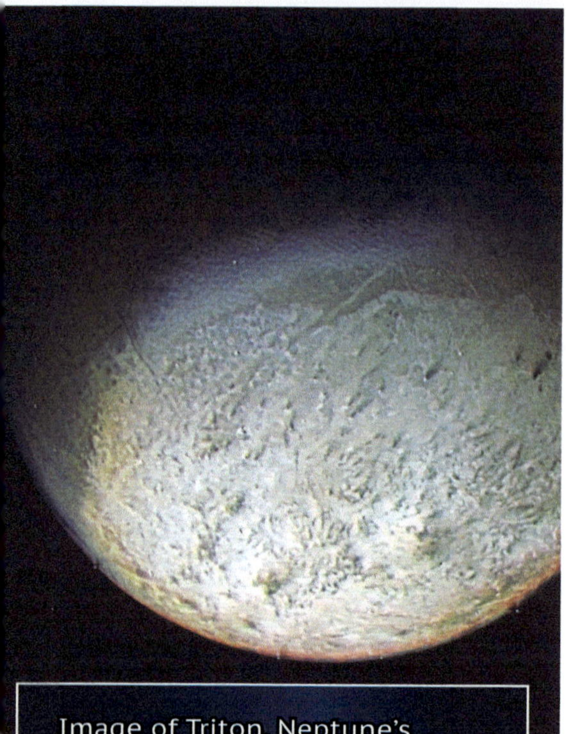

Image of Triton, Neptune's largest satellite, captured by a camera aboard Voyager 2, 1989.

i.e., they travel in prograde, nearly circular orbits that lie near Neptune's equatorial plane. In 2002–03 five additional tiny moons, estimated to be about 15–30 km (9–18 miles) in radius, were discovered in Earth-based observations. These are irregular, having highly eccentric orbits that are inclined at large angles to the planet's equator; three also orbit in the retrograde direction. Their mean distances from Neptune lie roughly between 15 million and 48 million km (9 million and 30 million miles), well outside the orbit of Nereid.

In 2013 a tiny moon, about 9 km (6 miles) in radius, was discovered in a Hubble Space Telescope image. Its orbit was tracked in archival images as far back as 2004, so it has the provisional designation S/2004 N1. It orbits between Larissa and Proteus, two moons discovered by Voyager.

Of Voyager's six discoveries, all but Proteus orbit Neptune in less time than it takes the planet to rotate.

Hence, to an observer positioned near Neptune's cloud tops, these five would appear to rise in the west and set in the east. Voyager observed two of its discoveries, Proteus and Larissa, closely enough to detect both their size and approximate shape. Both bodies are irregular in shape and appear to have heavily cratered surfaces. The sizes of the other four are estimated from a combination of distant images and their brightnesses, based on the assumption that they reflect about as much light as Proteus and Larissa—about 7 percent.

Proteus, with a mean radius of about 208 km (129 miles), is a little larger than Nereid, with a mean radius of about 170 km (106 miles). Because Proteus is so near to Neptune, however, scientists on Earth had been unable to detect it in the planet's glare. The other five moons are much smaller, each having a mean radius of less than 100 km (60 miles).

Voyager did not observe Nereid at close range, but data from the probe indicate that it has a nearly spherical shape. Voyager detected no large variations in brightness as Nereid rotated. Although the spacecraft was unable to determine a rotation period, the moon's highly elliptical orbit makes it unlikely that it is in synchronous rotation—i.e., that its rotation and orbital periods are equal. The rotation period of Triton is synchronous, and those of Neptune's other inner moons are probably synchronous or very nearly so.

Triton is similar in size, density, and surface composition to the dwarf planet Pluto. Its highly inclined, retrograde orbit suggests that it is a captured object, which perhaps formed originally, like Pluto, as an independent icy planetesimal in the outer solar system's Kuiper belt. Its original orbit would have been highly eccentric, but tidal interactions between Triton and Neptune—cyclic deformations in each body caused by the gravitational attraction of the other—eventually would have reshaped its path around Neptune into a circle.

The present orbits of Naiad through Proteus are probably very different from their original orbits, and these moons may be only fragments of the original bodies that formed with Neptune. Subsequent bombardment by Neptune-orbiting debris and by meteoroids from interplanetary space may have further altered their sizes, shapes, and orbits.

Neptune also has a population of Trojan asteroids that occupy the stable Lagrangian points 60° ahead (L4) and behind (L5) in its orbit around the Sun. The first Neptune Trojan, 2001 QR_{322}, was discovered in 2001. As of 2018, 17 Neptune Trojan asteroids are known; 13 are at L4, and 4 at L5.

Evidence that Neptune has one or more rings arose in the mid-1980s when stellar occultation studies from Earth occasionally showed a brief dip in the star's brightness just before or after the planet passed in front of it. Because dips were seen only in some studies and never symmetrically on both sides of the planet, scientists concluded that any rings present do not completely encircle Neptune but instead have the form of partial rings, or ring arcs.

Neptune's ring system, captured by Voyager 2 in two long-exposure backlit images made a few hours after the spacecraft's closest approach to the planet in August 1989.

Images from Voyager 2, however, revealed a system of six rings, each of which in fact fully surrounds Neptune. The putative arcs turned out to be bright regions in the outermost ring, named Adams, where the density of ring particles is particularly high. Although rings also encircle each of the other three giant planets, none displays the striking clumpiness of Adams.

Although the moon Galatea, which orbits just planetward of the inner edge of Adams, may gravitationally interact with the ring to trap ring particles temporarily in such arclike regions, collisions between ring particles should eventually spread the constituent material relatively uniformly around the ring. Consequently, it is suspected that the event that supplied the material for Adams's enigmatic arcs—perhaps the breakup of a small moon—occurred within the past few thousand years.

The other five known rings of Neptune—Galle, Le Verrier, Lassell, Arago, and Galatea, in order of increasing distance from the planet—lack the nonuniformity in density exhibited by Adams. Le Verrier, which is about 110 km (70 miles) in radial width, closely resembles the nonarc regions of Adams. Similar to the relationship between the moon Galatea and the ring Adams, the moon Despina orbits Neptune just planetward of the ring Le Verrier. Each moon may gravitationally repel particles near the inner edge of its respective ring, acting as a shepherd moon to keep ring material from spreading inward.

Galle, the innermost ring, is much broader and fainter than either Adams or Le Verrier, possibly owing to the absence of a nearby moon that could provide a strong shepherding effect. Lassell consists of a faint plateau of ring material that extends outward from Le Verrier about halfway to Adams. Arago is the name used to distinguish a narrow, relatively bright region at the outer edge of Lassell. Galatea is the name generally used to refer to a faint ring of material spread all along the orbit of the moon Galatea.

None of Neptune's rings was detected from scattering effects on Voyager's radio signal propagating through the rings, which indicates that they are nearly devoid of particles in the centimetre size range or larger. The fact that the rings were most visible in Voyager images when backlit by sunlight implies that they are largely populated by dust-sized particles, which scatter light forward much better than back toward the Sun and Earth. Their chemical makeup is not known, but, like the rings of Uranus, the surfaces of Neptune's ring particles (and possibly the particles in their entirety) may be composed of radiation-darkened methane ices.

Neptune's present rings may be much younger than the planet itself, perhaps substantially less than a million years. The present ring system may be markedly different from any that existed a million years ago. It is even possible that the next spacecraft to visit Neptune's rings will find a system greatly evolved from the one Voyager 2 imaged in 1989.

CONCLUSION

All of the outer planets—Jupiter, Neptune, Uranus, and Saturn—are much bigger than the inner planets, and Jupiter is more massive than the seven other planets combined. Unlike the inner planets, the outer planets have no solid surfaces. Their densities are less than twice the density of water. Jupiter and Saturn are composed mostly of hydrogen and helium in liquid and gaseous form, while Uranus and Neptune consist mainly of melted ices and molten rock, as well as hydrogen and helium. Each of the four has a massive atmosphere, a ring system, and many moons. The many moons of the outer planets are often unique and fascinating worlds in their own right and may offer the best hope of harboring extraterrestrial life in our own solar system.

Today, scientists are discovering a wealth of planets outside our own solar system, many of which are massive, much like our own outer planets. Between 5 and 10 percent of stars surveyed have planets at least 100 times as massive as Earth. The most massive planets that orbit their stars are made primarily of the two lightest elements, hydrogen and helium, as are Jupiter and Saturn. The term "Jupiters" is often used to describe these worlds. The lessons we are learning from the outer planets give us insight to the nature of those that are often much too far away to closely study.

GLOSSARY

accretion Growth by gradual buildup.

astronomical unit A unit of length effectively equal to the average, or mean, distance between Earth and the Sun, defined as 149,597,870.7 km (92,955,807.3 miles).

aurora A luminous phenomenon that consists of streamers or arches of light appearing in the upper atmosphere of a planet's magnetic polar regions and is caused by the emission of light from atoms excited by electrons accelerated along the planet's magnetic field lines.

convection Heat transfer, via liquid or gas, from one region to another.

Coriolis effect The deflection of a moving object that is a result of the Coriolis force.

density The mass of a unit volume of a material substance.

dipole A pair of electric charges or magnetic poles that are of equal magnitude but opposite sign or polarity, separated by a distance.

friction The force that resists relative motion between two bodies in contact.

gauss The centimetre-gram-second unit of magnetic flux density that is equal to 1×10^{-4} tesla.

interstellar Something that is located, taking place, or traveling among the stars.

Kelvin The base unit of temperature in the International System of Units that is equal to 1/273.16 of the Kelvin scale temperature of the triple point of water.

Kuiper belt A band of small celestial bodies beyond the orbit of Neptune from which many short-period comets are believed to originate.

magnetosphere A region surrounding a planet in which charged particles are trapped and their behaviour is dominated by the planet's magnetic field.

mass The property of a body that is a measure of its inertia and that is commonly taken as a measure of the amount of material it contains and causes it to have weight in a gravitational field.

nebula A mass of interstellar gas and dust.

orbit A path described by one body in its revolution about another.

planetesimal Any of numerous small celestial bodies that may have existed at an early stage of the development of the solar system.

prograde Direct motion of the planets around the Sun.

retrograde Moving backward or in an order that is opposite the usual.

silicate A salt or ester derived from a silicic acid.

solar wind Plasma continuously ejected from the Sun's surface into and through interplanetary space.

spectroscopy The production and investigation of spectra, a continuum of colour formed when a beam of white light is dispersed.

thermodynamics Physics that deals with the mechanical action or relations of heat.

tidal force The effect of the stretching of a body toward the centre of mass of another body due to the gradient in strength of the gravitational field.

velocity The rate of change of position along a straight line with respect to time.

GIANT JUPITER

The Jovian system—the planet Jupiter and its moons, magnetosphere, and rings—is discussed in detail and compared with the other giant planets in (in order of increasing difficulty) J. Kelly Beatty, Carolyn Collins Petersen, and Andrew Chaikin, *The New Solar System*, 4th ed. (1999); David Morrison and Tobias Owen, *The Planetary System*, 3rd ed. (2003); and Imke de Pater and Jack J. Lissauer, *Planetary Sciences* (2001). A comprehensive, popular-level review of knowledge of the Jovian system, including early results from the Galileo space probe, is Reta Beebe, *Jupiter: The Giant Planet*, 2nd ed. (1997). Jupiter's moons are discussed in the context of all the moons of the outer solar system in David A. Rothery, *Satellites of the Outer Planets: Worlds in Their Own Right*, 2nd ed. (1999). Detailed descriptions of the Galileo mission and its findings are provided in David M. Harland, *Jupiter Odyssey: The Story of NASA's Galileo Mission* (2000); and Daniel Fischer, *Mission Jupiter: The Spectacular Journey of the Galileo Spacecraft* (2001). The original reference for visual observations of Jupiter with telescopes of moderate size is Bertrand M. Peek, *The Planet Jupiter*, rev. by Patrick Moore (1981). A more recent account that includes results from the Voyager space probes is John H. Rogers, *The Giant Planet Jupiter* (1995). Details regarding the Voyager missions may be found in David Morrison and Jane Samz, *Voyage to Jupiter* (1980).

SATURN: THE JEWEL OF THE SOLAR SYSTEM

J. Kelly Beatty, Carolyn Collins Petersen, and Andrew Chaikin (eds.), *The New Solar System*, 4th ed. (1999), contains chapters written by experts for nonscientists about the atmosphere, interior, rings, and moons of Saturn and the other giant planets. A nontechnical description of the Cassini-Huygens mission is given in Linda J. Spilker (ed.), *Passage to a Ringed World: The Cassini-Huygens Mission to Saturn and Titan* (1997). More-advanced treatments of the Saturnian system, written by specialists, are contained in Michele K. Dougherty, Larry W. Esposito, and Stamatios M. Krimigis (eds.), *Saturn from Cassini-Huygens* (2009). Articles in scientific journals include *Science*, 327(5972):1476–79 (March 19, 2010), a review of the Cassini results regarding the atmosphere, ionosphere, and magnetosphere; *Science*, 307 (5713):1222–76 (Feb. 25, 2005), a special section of reports devoted to early Cassini results; and *Science*, 311(5766):1388–1428 (March 10, 2006), a special section of reports devoted to Cassini findings regarding Saturn's moon Enceladus.

URANUS: AN ICE GIANT

Ellis D. Miner and Randii R. Wessen, *Neptune: The Planet, Rings, and Satellites* (2001), is a popular work that updates the knowledge of Neptune and its system following the 1989 encounter of Voyager 2. J. Kelly Beatty, Carolyn Collins Petersen, and Andrew Chaikin (eds.), *The New Solar System*, 4th ed. (1999), contains chapters written by experts for nonscientists about the atmosphere, interior, rings, and moons of Neptune and the other giant planets. By far the most comprehensive and current treatise on Neptune is Dale P. Cruikshank (ed.), *Neptune and Triton* (1995). A set of articles in *Science*, 246(4936):1417–1501 (December 15, 1989), comprises the initial report of the Voyager findings at Neptune; more detailed reports of the findings are in a set of articles in *Journal of Geophysical Research, Supplement*, 96:18,903–19,268 (October 30, 1991); and in Eric Burgess, *Far Encounter: The Neptune System* (1991), a popular work that also contains some discussion of Pluto. Patrick Moore, *The Planet Neptune: An Historical Survey Before Voyager*, 2nd ed. (1996), provides a good summary of pre-Voyager knowledge of the planet. Mark Littmann, *Planets Beyond: Discovering the Outer Solar System*, updated and rev. ed. (1990, reissued 2004), chronicles the history of the discovery of Uranus, Neptune, and Pluto.

BIG, BLUE NEPTUNE

J. Kelly Beatty, Carolyn Collins Petersen, and Andrew Chaikin (eds.), *The New Solar System*, 4th ed. (1999), contains numerous photographs and 28 chapters written by specialists on all aspects of solar system science, including the Uranian system and the systems of the other giant planets. A.P. Ingersoll, "Uranus," *Scientific American*, 256(1):38–45 (January 1987), provides an introductory review article with illustrations and diagrams. Garry E. Hunt and Patrick Moore, *Atlas of Uranus* (1989), offers an in-depth introduction. The first reports of Voyager 2's encounter written by the Voyager scientists are included in a set of 12 articles in *Science*, 233(4759):39–109 (July 4, 1986), which contains most of the best images of the planet, its moons, and its rings. Jay T. Bergstralh, Ellis D. Miner, and Mildred Shapley Matthews (eds.), *Uranus* (1991), is the definitive reference work on the subject, with chapters written by specialists in the field. Ellis D. Miner, *Uranus: The Planet, Rings, and Satellites*, 2nd ed. (1998), reviews modern knowledge of the planet, with much background information on the Voyager mission. Garry E. Hunt (ed.), *Uranus and the Outer Planets* (1982), a pre-Voyager summary dealing almost exclusively with Uranus, contains some interesting historical chapters. Eric Burgess, *Uranus and Neptune: The Distant Giants* (1988), also focuses primarily on Uranus. Mark Littmann, *Planets Beyond: Discovering the Outer Solar System*, updated and rev. ed. (1990, reissued 2004), chronicles the history of the discoveries of Uranus, Neptune, and Pluto.

INDEX

R

S

T

U

V